Anonymous

Hereward, the Saxon Patriot

A history of his life and character, with a record of his ancestors and descendants, A. D. 445 to A. D. 1896

Anonymous

Hereward, the Saxon Patriot
A history of his life and character, with a record of his ancestors and descendants, A. D. 445 to A. D. 1896

ISBN/EAN: 9783337094560

Printed in Europe, USA, Canada, Australia, Japan

Cover: Foto ©ninafisch / pixelio.de

More available books at **www.hansebooks.com**

HEREWARD

The Saxon Patriot:

A HISTORY OF HIS LIFE AND CHARACTER, WITH A RECORD OF HIS ANCESTORS AND DESCENDANTS, A.D. 445 TO A.D. 1896.

BY

LIEUTENANT-GENERAL HARWARD.

> 'What man is he that boasts of fleshly might,
> And vain assurance of mortality?'
>
> * * * * *
>
> 'Ne let the man ascribe it to his skill
> That thorough grace hath gained Victory.
> If any strength we have, it is to ill;
> But all the good is God's, both power, and eke will.'
>
> SPENSER'S *Faerie Queene*, Canto X.

LONDON:
ELLIOT STOCK, 62, PATERNOSTER ROW, E.C.
1896.

Preface.

THE story of the lives of our national heroes cannot fail to excite the sympathy & interest of Englishmen, & few are more entitled to the respect & honour of their countrymen than Hereward. Hitherto the memory of this mighty man has been too much disregarded; & in these pages an attempt has been made to recall the history, origin, & lineage of a brave hero, who tried to do his duty to his country in troublous & disastrous days, to whom failure & despair were unknown, & the record of whose unrivalled deeds may be traced in every subsequent effort which Englishmen have made to maintain & extend their freedom by patriotic sacrifice for their country's welfare.

To rescue from oblivion the memory of Hereward is our endeavour. We shall examine the scanty records of mediæval history, & carefully analyze the statements of subsequent commentators. The novel of the Rev. Charles Kingsley is the best known of our modern authorities, but the work is full of inaccuracies, of which the title-page is a standing witness, wherein the author surnames Hereward "the Wake," & calls him the last of the English. The history of Hereward under the Danish name of "*Harold Leurickson,*" published at Copenhagen, is a far truer record; but the traditions of this hero are scanty, & the modern authorities on which they are based cannot be accepted without hesitation. But we shall endeavour to record all that can be ascertained with probability.

His place in history is important. That Hereward's patriotic action insured the respect of the Norman Conqueror is proved by the restitution of many of his family estates, & whatever amelioration of their condition the English obtained from their Norman conquerors was due to the energy & patriotism of Hereward. His character, too, is remarkable, & in it we find the germ of that self-reliant courage to which are due the greatness & freedom of our country.

We have endeavoured also to determine what families have a right to trace their descent from Hereward, & that branch of our inquiry is not without some personal interest, as we ourselves claim him as our illustrious ancestor :

"*Attollens humero famamque & fata nepotum.*"[1]

In conclusion, we trust that these records may help to elucidate some obscure facts in the history of the times of Hereward, & to preserve the memory of one who wrought mighty deeds for England in the brave days of old, & was the forerunner of many illustrious heroes who have lived & died for their country's weal, & have proved themselves worthy of the name of Englishmen.

[1] *Æneid*, viii. 731.

Table of Contents and Synopsis.

	PAGE
PREFACE - - - - - - - -	V

CHAPTER I.

Introduction.—An ill-used hero—Apology for authorship—Incompleteness of material—Confusion of facts in histories of the Middle Ages—A word in deprecation of criticism - - 1

CHAPTER II.

Hereward's ancestral record.—Remote origin of the family—Early settlements in Britain—System of Saxon colonization—A Saxon town—Domestic life in the sixth century—Intermarriage with Christianized Danes—Herewald, Bishop of Sherburne, 690 A.D.—Descent of Hereward from the Earls of Mercia - - - 7

CHAPTER III.

Life of Hereward.—Boyhood, exile, and marriage—Undoubted records of Domesday Book—Hereward's manly character, and love of arms and sports—Trained for knighthood—Unpopularity with the ascetic King Edward and his French Court—Jealousy of Godwin's sons —Exiled life in Flanders—Marries Torfrida—Returns to England 16

CHAPTER IV.

Life of Hereward continued.—The Camp of Refuge—Hereward knighted —Saxon struggle for hearth and home—The camp in the Fens— Edwin and Morcar—William establishes headquarters at the Castle of Cambridge—Leads his army against Hereward: his failure and repulse—Military genius of Hereward—Treachery of the monks—Hereward moves camp to the woods of Bourne— Captures Ivo de Taillebois—Makes terms with William—Good Bishop Wulfstan—His ward, the Lady Ælfthryth - - 33

CHAPTER V.

Life of Hereward concluded.—An interval of peace—The campaign in Maine—Hereward in command of English troops—Curious details in Saxon Chronicle of his alleged death by violence—His honourable character—Record of the "Great Book of Ely"—Leaves descendants in Warwickshire and Norfolk — His death probably peaceful - - - - - - - 44

CHAPTER VI.

Etymology and orthography of Hereward.—Literary changes—Test of legitimate modifications—Proof from contemporary records, coins, inscriptions—Gothic or Scandinavian origin of the name—Referred to by Tacitus—Variations admissible—Saxon and Danish differences - - - - - - - 50

CHAPTER VII.

Doubtful claimants of the lineage.—Names derived from Norman offices—Claim of the Dukes of Norfolk and families of Howard—Claims of the late Duke of Buckingham, Lord Palmerston, Sir Grenville Temple, and Sir Herwald Wake considered inadmissible—Fictitious records in Heralds' Visitations - - - 57

CHAPTER VIII.

The recorded evidence of heraldry.—Classical reference to armorial bearings—Early customs of Heraldry in England—Saxon disabilities after the Norman Conquest—The Herewards' social position — Caprice in selecting heraldic devices — Ten various shields of arms recorded as borne by Herewards, Herwards, or Harwards - - - - - - - 65

CHAPTER IX.

The Herewards after the Norman Conquest.—Better government by Henry II.—The Hereward family policy—Hold aloof from internecine or revolutionary wars—The Barons' War—The Commonwealth—True patriotism exemplified—Records of Blomefield, Dugdale, Nash, and Grazebrook—Pedigrees in Heralds' College—Warwickshire branch settle in Worcestershire - - - 75

CHAPTER X.

Genealogical outline.—Distinctive marks of family—Key tables—Authorities for direct descent recapitulated—Authorities consulted—Present memoir an initial base only—Danish connection — Custom of hereditary descent — Untitled nobility — Family history 600 A.D. to 1066 A.D.—Sketches of Warwickshire and Norfolk branches—Norfolk line becomes extinct—Warwickshire branch migrates into Worcestershire - - - - 81

APPENDICES - - - - - - - - 99

Key Tables.

		PAGE
(A)	DIRECT LINE OF HEREWARD TO THE NORMAN CONQUEST	88
(B)	WARWICKSHIRE BRANCH PEDIGREE OF HEREWARD	89
(C)	SKETCH PEDIGREE OF ROUMARA OF REVESBY	92
(D)	THREE BRANCHES OF HEREWARD, OR HARWARD	93
(E)	THE HEREWARDS IN NORFOLK	94
(F)	HARWARD, OR HEREWARD, OF HARTLEBURY, CO. WIGORN	95
(G)	KEY TABLE OF MICHAEL HARWARD, ESQ., OF HARTLEBURY, 1728 TO 1807	96
(H)	KEY TABLE OF HARWARD OF HARVINGTON, CO. WIGORN	97
(I)	KEY TABLE OF REV. JNO. HARWARD, OF HARTLEBURY, 1760 TO 1855	98

ERRATA.

Page 6, line 1, *for* " Bowme " *read* " Bourne."
 ,, 52   ,, 25, their should be written l , not ſ.
 ,, 70   ,, 10, insert "a" before "fesse."
 ,, 70   ,, 10, *for* "chequey" *read* "chequy."
 ,, 70, note [1], line 5, *for* " Acoulonthos " *read* " Acoulouthos."
 ,, 71, line 15, *for* " Chesten " *read* " Cheston."
 ,, 72   ,, 20, *for* " Magestri " *read* " Magistri."
 ,, 88   ,, 7 from bottom, *for* " Alfryth " *read* " Ælfthryth."

(*Anglice:* " Pen he took with fingers, and wrote on book-skin, and the true words set together.")

NGLAND has never failed to produce at least one hero to grace every achievement in arms which has added glory and renown to our country. National historians, true to the traditions they expound, are averse to laying too much stress upon individual prowess, rightly concluding that when Englishmen are banded together in defence of national honour, all are prepared to make equal sacrifice; and though success may be achieved in a greater degree by one only, honour is equally due to all.

Herewardi Arbor Gentis.

Chapter j.

Introduction.

"First in the race that led to glory's goal."
BYRON.

"fetheren he nom mid fingren,
& fiede on boc-felle,
& tha sothe word
sette to-gadere."
LAYAMON—*Origines Britanniæ*, vol. i., p. 3.

(*Anglice :* "Pen he took with fingers, and wrote on book-skin, and the true words set together.")

NGLAND has never failed to produce at least one hero to grace every achievement in arms which has added glory and renown to our country. National historians, true to the traditions they expound, are averse to laying too much stress upon individual prowess, rightly concluding that when Englishmen are banded together in defence of national honour, all are prepared to make equal sacrifice ; and though success may be achieved in a greater degree by one only, honour is equally due to all.

Hereward, the Saxon patriot, has met with even a harsher fate than ordinary British heroes. He has not only been allowed to fall into oblivion, but for many generations his race was impoverished, marked and proscribed, and the descendants of the Norman usurpers have even demeaned themselves to covet the empty honour of his name. So late as Tudor days it would have been hazardous to bring Hereward's name and fame, and his connection with the royal Saxon house, too prominently forward; so his descendants lived in peace with their neighbours, were liberal landlords and respected citizens, never ceasing their connection with the Church, to which they contributed many dignitaries and working clergy up to the present day.

Their motto has been:

> "manus hoc inimica tyrannis
> Ense petit placidam sub libertate quietem."
> (This hand, to tyrants hostile ever,
> Grasps the sword that makes us free,
> And seeks, intent our bonds to sever,
> Gentle rest in liberty.)

Hitherto it has not been suggested that Hereward's family history should supplement the hiatus in our national archives, but we now propose to collect the valuable records available in manuscripts and ancient muniments, the combined treasures of the British Museum and the Record Office,[1] and eventually to construct a satisfactory and accurate memorial of the patriot chief and his people. We can only claim for these pages a good intention to initiate a work of both public and private interest, and we sincerely trust that the completion of the task will devolve upon more able and expert hands than our own. But in the meantime it is better to take the work in hand than to again postpone it, for lack of complete material, for an indefinite period.

We must also protect ourselves, as representing the line of Hereward, against a charge of egoism, in maintaining our

---

[1] Also in episcopal registers, chartularies and MSS. relating to the abbeys and other religious houses, records of the King's Courts, wills and conveyances, and other historical matter relating to Hereward, his kinsmen, and their estates.

Introduction. 3

rights of lineage against all comers. This we have been compelled to do by the merciless, and, we fear, unscrupulous appropriations by persons with no rational claim to the lineage of Hereward. It is to be regretted there is not now a court of honour with power to purge such publications as peerages and cognate works emanating from quasi-heraldic offices from inaccuracies and indefensible statements.

The extraordinary desire evinced by newly-created peers who cannot boast of any exalted lineage to establish a historical ancestry is the chief cause of this trifling with national records.

The College of Arms should be a working instead of an idle institution; and until it is thoroughly reorganized and placed under different control, the public cannot expect the advantage which might be derived from it. A representative from that office would find constant employment in searching the muniments available, and in verifying or exposing the statements at present recorded in the Earl Marshal's books.

As a family rather than a public history, we feel at liberty to place before our readers incidents of slight importance or interest, with the hope they may become connecting links in the chain of evidence, or clues to aid in the devolution of a somewhat tangled web.

Lord Macaulay says "History begins in novel and ends in essay," and making due allowance for qualifications and exceptions to this rule, it seems a fair definition of the ordinary scope of history in literature; and when the historical essayist has to write of matters 800 years after the event, a third factor must be dealt with, and reason steps in to keep the balance. Facts at a distance are apt to become hazy, and the more numerous the novels and essays from which our facts are to be evolved, the more difficult becomes the task of separating the wheat from the chaff, and in eliminating incidents which the light of subsequent history assures us to be probable, from others which the same influence convinces us are due to the ignorance and prejudice of bygone ages, being intrinsically improbable and irreconcilable with assured facts.

The halo of romance must necessarily enshrine the memory

of such a *preux chevalier* as Hereward. A patriot and a hero, he was yet one of a conquered race, and the appointment of Norman abbots and priors would not tend to encourage the monastic writers of Saxon history.

The chronicles have not, however, been silent. The difficulty is to separate the facts founded upon history from the legends and fictions inherent in oral testimony and *post facto* records. Professor Freeman somewhat unjustifiably rejects every record of Hereward unconfirmed by his favourite writers, Florence of Worcester and Orderic, though the latter was too young to have known personally the events of the early Norman period. But, throughout the history of the Norman Conquest, Freeman does not hesitate to give his version of important historical events unsupported in some instances by better authority than a French romance or *post facto* writer. The author of the "De Hyda," another favourite of Freeman's, clearly a Norman, cannot say sufficiently evil things of Hereward. His combat with Frederick Warren in wager by battle is described as "*inter cœtera scelera sua*," and as "*fraudibus circumventum*," whereas Hereward's undoubted bravery completely falsifies such aspersions.

If unsupported testimony should be received with caution, still less should any record be rejected until it is proved absolutely untrustworthy. Especial reference is made to the chronicle of the so-called "False Ingulph," who has been quoted as an authority by law-writers to the present day. Surely something can be gained from him?[1]

[1] Critics have established the fact to their own content that the record of Croyland is not the genuine work of the Abbot Ingulph, sometime secretary to William, but the composition of an unauthorized scribe who assumed Ingulph's name.

It is, however, a remarkable comment upon this criticism that the law writers of later periods have on several occasions quoted the authority of Ingulph, notably to prove that Domesday Book was the work of William, and not of Edward the Confessor, as sometimes alleged. The authority of Ingulph is also adduced to show the change made by the Normans after the Conquest in the executions of deeds (*faits*): "Normanni cheirographorum confectionem cum crucibus aureis, et aliis signaculis sacris in Anglia firmari solitam in cærâ impressâ mutant, modumque scribendo Anglicum rejiciunt." ("The Normans do change the making of writings, which were wont to be firmed in England

Introduction. 5

The state of barbarism, too, in which the Normans found England at the Conquest was characterized not more by the priest-ridden government of Edward the Confessor than by the dearth of credible histories. While correct and polished writers like Herodotus and Tacitus had enlightened Eastern Europe, our literature betrayed the ignorance and uncouthness of our Saxon progenitors. In the result we have to grope our way in semi-darkness; and all these various causes add greatly to the difficulties of investigation.

No English historian has made any effort to ascertain whether Hereward of Ely had either ancestors or descendants. We propose to open up such sources of information as are available. Much stress has been laid upon the fact that Hereward's daughter, Torfrida, married Hugh de Evermue, Lord of Deeping, county Lincoln, sometime tenant of Here-

---

with Crosses of gold, and other holy signes, into the pinning waxe, and they reject also the manner of the English writing.") It seems as unwise to reject Ingulph or other doubtful authority, as it does to accept such an authority without careful consideration.

At the period of the Norman Conquest even the family records of the Duke of Normandy and his cotemporaries were in the most hazy condition. Who can tell the relationship of Ghesbod and Gundreda to William I., or that of Richard Guett, the benefactor of Bermondsey, and alleged brother of the Countess Warren? Who can say whether there was or was not any issue of Eustace, Count of Boulogne, by Goda his wife, daughter of Ethelred II.? The existence of his three sons by his second marriage with Ida, daughter of the Duke of Lorraine, would not have been recorded had not his second son become the celebrated Godfrey of Bouillon, King of Jerusalem.

Beyond the fact that he died in September, 1087, at about the age of sixty, we have little or no assured account of William. The date of his birth is unknown, or the history of his mother's family, except that her name was Arlotte, or Herleve, the daughter of "a tanner of Falaise" (name unknown), and that she was not married to William's father. Even the evidence of Duke Robert's marriage to Matilda is unreliable. William's mother, Arlotte, appears to have been made over to Herluin de Conteville, or Gilbert de Crepon, when Duke Robert married Estrith, sister of Canute, and widow of Ulf, a Dane.

If, then, the pages of public and private history were so barren of facts and details, it is only by the closest research amongst cotemporary records, in microscopic detail, that we can find clues of evidence to the events of the time and the history of the people. The extraordinary manipulation and falsification which the most important historical documents have undergone, such as the Roll of Battle Abbey, is enough to check the most ardent student of archaic lore.

ward's estate and birthplace of Brune, or Bowme, and conclude that he had no heirs male. As Torfrida married a Norman instead of one of her own race, the event obtained more notoriety; but there is certainly no conclusive proof of the absence of a male heir, and distinct proof of the existence of Herewards in the next century related to the renowned exile and patriot, as proved by the "Liber Ecclesiæ Eliensis." Torfrida may have been the only issue of the first marriage in Flanders, and her mother may not have been of purely Saxon parentage; but it is probable Hereward's male descendants came from his second marriage with the Saxon lady Aelfthryth.

It will be seen that one object of this discussion is to call in question the claims of some of those who aspire to kinship with Hereward and his descendants. We shall be able to establish valid grounds for a searching inquiry into such doubtful claims, while we shall endeavour to show what families have a right to trace their descent from so distinguished an ancestor. We who love to trace the lives of our ancestors back through their generations, to recount their virtues and their heroic deeds, may be able to unravel the intricacies of the times in which their lot was cast, and to aid not immaterially in the development of historical truth.

Chapter ij.

Hereward's Ancestors.

" From the barred visor of Antiquity
Reflected shines the eternal light of Truth
As from a mirror."
LONGFELLOW.

OME of the noble lords who desire to trace their ancestry to the great Saxon patriot evidently imagine that he was a spontaneous creation. Like most of us, he had forefathers, and although his pedigree is naturally incomplete, it is by no means impossible to trace an outline of the movements and vicissitudes of the family of Hereward from a very early period.

The etymology of Hereward assures us that the name represented a military officer, holding large and important functions in war, and corresponding rank and position. It is equally certain from the spelling of the word that it came straight from Germany without touch from Dane or Jute. It is quite possible to carry speculation back to a remote period when a Harvard may have come with a band of Northmen to the Low Countries, and so into Germany.

In one of the Sagas Thorvard is mentioned as a mythical hero. The Batavian prince mentioned by Tacitus, Chariovalda or Harivald, is the oldest and most famous of the family mentioned in history, but the name is of Gothic origin and of great antiquity. The Norman cry for justice, "Haro!"[1] still used in the Channel Islands, is probably an appeal to an old Celtic god. The sword has always been held to be an emblem of justice, as well as the scales. At Queen Victoria's coronation the Duke of Wellington, carrying the sword, fulfilled the ancient Saxon office of Heornvard, or Hereward, the warden of the sword. The rank of Heretoga was sometimes accorded to a Saxon earl, or earldorman, corresponding to "herzog" in German, finally translated "dux" in Latin, "duke" in English. It had a political and territorial signification. The Hereward, or sword-guardian, may have been an officer in charge of Woden's Wagon, which always accompanied a Teutonic army, with judicial as well as military functions. He may, however, have been descended from Ariovistus, the warlike chief of the Suevi, who were one and all a race of soldiers and held the foremost place amongst the Alemanni, colonizing in France and Lusitania, and doubtless in England also. Ariovistus resembled Hereward in many points of character, in fearlessness, skill in arms, and contempt of his enemy.[2] Ariovistus might be translated Herefurst.

Leaving this speculation for future discussion, we have the undoubted fact that at some period after the Roman Hegira a Saxon leader named Hereward landed in England at the

[1] Har, or Haro, was an ancient name of Woden.

[2] Ariovistus, chief of the Suevi B.C. 56. It does not seem impossible to translate Ariovistus into Hereward. They are both leaders in war, and disciples of Mars or Woden. The Suevi were the best and most patriotic tribe of Germany. They colonized largely as far as Portugal in the south. They came from the country between the Elbe and the Vistula. Ariovistus was defeated only by Julius Cæsar and the indomitable tenth legion. In character he much resembled Hereward. He refused to attend Cæsar when summoned, saying, "If his business required it, he should come to him." He was a man of resource and strategy and a skilful soldier, like Hereward. He not only created a profound panic in Cæsar's army, but communicated with leading patricians at Rome, and then told Cæsar that, although his death was desired at Rome, he would be his friend, and be responsible for the good government of Gaul. He was, however, defeated by Cæsar, though worthy to have been the ancestor of Hereward. He was certainly a Teuton, though bearing a name derived from the Greek, and indicating a soldier.

Hereward became a personal name though derived from an office, as Chancellor, King, Knight, and many others to this day.

Hereward's Ancestors.

old Roman port near Pevensey, and with his followers marched through the forest of Andredes-weald, until he arrived on the northern slope of the Surrey hills, when he established his first settlement, known as Herewardesleag, and afterwards as Harwardsley, abbreviated to Horley, still a town in Surrey. No Saxon settlement could be formed with less than ten families, whence it was called "tything." But Horley was a hundred, and that number of families must have accompanied their chief to England and settled at Horley.[1] The position was no doubt convenient on the highroad to London and St. Albans and the Watling Street.[2] Still, a position so near the coast, though it had its

[1] Manning and Bray's "History of the County of Surrey" mentions Horley Manor. It afterwards belonged to the Abbey of Chertsey, and now to Christ's Hospital. "A large common, leag, or leah, from very ancient times called Donderfield or Thunderfield (German, the underfield), lies partly in this parish. Near the south-east border of it is a piece of ground, part of Harrowsley, *i.e.*, Harwardesley Manor, containing about two acres called Thunderfield Castle," probably the ancient Hereward stronghold (see Horne). In the reign of Henry III. the Countess of Warren held a quarter of a knight's fee in Herewoldesley of the honor of Clare. In 23rd Ed. III., 1350, the Priory of Bishopsgate held one-third of a knight's fee in Herewardeslee. 9th Rich. II., 1386, Reginald de Cobham, of Kent, granted to John Piers an annual rent of eight marcs from his manor of Herewardesle, also spelt Harrowsley and Haroldislegh. The author of "Lincolnshire and the Danes" derives Thunderfield from Thor, the Celtic god, and this is not improbable.

[2] According to the Saxon chronicles, three ships with armed Saxons and Danes, under the reputed leadership of Hengist and Horsa, landed on the east coast of Britain in A.D. 449. They came as friends and allies at the invitation of Vortigern, or Vurtherm,* who was then *de facto* King of Britain. His senate or council, the origin of the witangemote, concurred in the invitation, as the predatory Picts and Irish (Scots) had terribly harried the British people.

The new-comers soon took the field against the aggressors, and gained a complete victory over them. Finding themselves masters of the situation, they obtained the consent of Vortigern to increase their number, and sent such an account of the fertility of the country, and of the cowardice and indolence of the Britons, as induced their countrymen to reinforce them with a considerable fleet and army. Differences naturally arose between the Britons and the Saxons, the latter claiming on the strength of their numbers and position a larger share of provisions and plunder than they were justly entitled

* Modern "Wurtheimer."

advantages, must have been liable at times to unwelcome visitors, and as the Saxon settlement in Britain increased, a move was made towards the interior, and a second settlement of the same name, now called Horley, was formed in

to. From this time war and bloodshed ensued between the allies, and in A.D. 457 we find that the original party of Saxons and Danes under Hengist were masters of Kent as well as of a part of the east coast, although Pevensey Castle and the western country was still in possession of the Britons. The Isle of Thanet had been assigned to Hengist by Vortigern, on his arrival. During the next twenty years war was carried on, and the Britons repulsed with general slaughter.

In A.D. 477 the first landing on the south coast appears to have been made near Pevensey, in Sussex, by Ælla, with his three sons, and a large party of Saxon colonists. They were soon followed by Cerdic (Cedric) and his son Cynric, who landed further west at Charford, near Fordingbridge, in Hampshire.

The effect of this movement was to turn the flank of the Britons, and to place the whole of Sussex, as well as Kent, in the hands of the Saxons, who began to form a regular settlement in tythings and hundreds. Hengist had been elected King of Kent, and Ælla and Assa undertook to drive the Britons out of Sussex and Hants. A great battle—in which the Hereward hundred doubtless bore a part—was fought at Andredes-leag, in front of the great forest extending nearly a hundred miles through the wealds of Kent and Sussex. The Britons were scattered in flight with much slaughter and great spoils to the victors.

This district was so completely occupied by the Saxons that it was ever afterwards called Saxony, or Seaxe, the name being afterwards modified to Suth Seaxe, or Sussex, to distinguish it from other Saxon colonies in Britain, which was now rapidly becoming England. There is ample evidence to show that the first Hereward who arrived in England was of the Sussex party, and he probably landed in A.D. 477, or he may have joined Ælla subsequently, but prior to A.D. 492, when Pevensey Castle was besieged and taken, and the garrison put to the sword; for so long as the Britons remained in possession of this important stronghold, the Saxon colonists in Sussex were liable to attack, and must have remained on the defensive.

The Saxon settlement was then completed, and lands assigned to Hereward and his retainers at Horley, in Surrey, at that time quite an advanced position, and requiring a skilful warrior to guard it. Thus it is clear that before the end of the fifth century the first Hereward settlement was formed. The name is also attached to some lands in Sussex, near East Grinstead, at Fork Common, still called Herewards, and Hayward's Heath, near Brighton, probably commemorates a camp at one time occupied by Hereward's band of warriors. It indicates very early settlement, as all suitable sites in the south of England were occupied by early Saxon colonists immediately after the departure of the Roman troops.

Hereward's Ancestors.

Oxfordshire on the borders of Warwickshire,[1] sixteen miles south-west of Weedon. The position was well chosen, strategically, being near the Watlinge Street, but a few miles off the direct road. It does not appear ever to have become a place of as much note as the Surrey settlement, but it established the family in Mercia, in which province they at once took an influential part, until they occupied the almost regal position of earls. As a matter of fact, the chief of the party led by Hereward had, according to Teutonic usage, held the authority and power of an under-king over his own tribe.[2] With the aid of Mr. Wright's description, it is easy to call to mind such a settlement. The thatched cottages of timber and plaster, or "wattle and dab," lined with skins and furs, and carpeted with rushes, with perhaps a fortified mound on the nearest hill for defence. The freemen, aided by their serfs, engaged in husbandry or bargained with their neighbours for wool, homespun, or cattle, corn, or cheese — a barter more common than a purchase, and in the latter case such a production of curious Roman, British, and Saxon coin, of leather, copper, tin and silver, as would make the fortune of a modern numismatist. An occasional visit from a worthy monk who taught and preached filled up one day in the week; while relaxation was found in the exercise of arms, a bout at

[1] The settlement of the clan extended in this and in the neighbouring counties. In the Domesday of Edward the Confessor Hereward had lands at Merstone, Marston Jabbet, in Warwickshire, and Barnard and Ladbroke (Ladbroc) in the same county, besides a knight's fee at Evenlode, in Worcestershire. These lands were held *in capite* in King Edward's time, but were given by William to one Meulan, or Mellent, a free-lance and so-called count, as over-lord. He was the alleged ancestor of the Dukes of Hamilton.

[2] "Teutonic society was essentially aristocratic, the heads of clans or tribes selecting land which was occupied by their families and followers, and which descended as a freehold. Anglo-Saxon landowners were lords of the soil and of the people on their own allotment. They founded territorial boundaries amongst themselves, known as hundreds, shires, etc., to enable them to manage their own affairs, and to administer justice. *The landowner acknowledged his subjection to the chief under whom he had come into the island, and the latter became king or under-king of that province.* The old Roman and mixed population of the towns still occupied the old houses under the Saxon lord. The latter objected to occupy the Roman houses, preferring to build houses for themselves of timber, thatch and plaster."—Wright's "The Celt, Roman, and Saxon."

quarter-staff, shooting at a mark with long or crossbow, training a hawk or hound for the pursuit of game, then public property, or even in chopping timber or cutting turf for fuel. The head of the tribe, under the nearest tree, administered justice in patriarchal fashion, saw to the defences, and inspected and bought arms or other appliances for husbandry or defence. Truly a simple but not a distasteful life to lead in time of peace. In war the tribe had to fight for hearth and home, or for their lord's quarrel; women and children listened with bated breath for news from the wars, and sometimes trembled, not without reason.

Now and again the chief was called upon to attend a witangemote, or to wait upon his sovereign in a neighbouring shire, when he met the earl, bishop, abbot, and other functionaries. His tale of men-at-arms was counted, his report made to the king, and perhaps a request preferred for a marriage, or office; and to the abbot for a monk to be permanently sent to his "tun"[1] (town), or to place a son who was fond of learning in the monastery for instruction.

About 690 A.D., a Hereward was sent presumably to Canterbury, near the Surrey estate, where he had the advantage of study under the learned Abbot Hadrian, who, from his own eminence, had imparted a high character for learning and divinity to St. Augustine's Abbey. The future co-ordinate Bishop of Winchester may have been educated at Malmesbury or Glastonbury, but there is not the same reason for the conjecture. Hereward, or Herewald, as Bede has recorded it, was ordained Bishop of Sherborne in 736 A.D.,[2] and of good birth, well educated, with a sacred mission to perform, he could hardly fail to be an acceptable adviser to Ethelhard, successor to Ina, King of the West Saxons. For nearly fifty years he administered the diocese, but there are few records of his work. He signed charters, attended councils, and aided the evangelization of the Western pagans,

---

[1] *Tún* was in its original sense the hedge or fence by which the enclosed leag or demesne was surrounded, and soon came to mean the farm itself, and eventually a collection of houses forming a complete settlement.

[2] The See of Winchester was then divided into the two bishoprics of Winchester and Sherborne.

besides strengthening the organization of his diocese, and enlarging the number of his communicants and congregations.

The Hereward family settled in Oxfordshire had raised themselves to eminence in the kingdom of Mercia before Egbert united the Saxon kingdoms under one crown. Leofric, the first chief recorded in the annals of Croyland and Coventry, was Earl of Leicester in 745 A.D.; his son Algar was created Earl of Lincoln,[1] and the Earldom of Hereford was also conferred upon their descendants, until Leofric III. became lord of the marches and Earl of Chester, with a residence at Hedoine, now Hawarden, Castle, and ultimately Earl of Mercia, 975-1057.[2] Authorities are not agreed that Hereward's father, Leofric, Lord of Bourne, in Lincolnshire, and the Earl of Mercia were one and the same, but there is such strong evidence in favour of this contention recorded in Domesday, that I feel no hesitation in adopting it. This pedigree, prior to the Norman Conquest, will be shown in a later chapter giving a Genealogical Outline of Hereward's Ancestors and Descendants.

The Herewards, or Harwards, have always supported the Anglican Church. Leofric built and endowed many abbeys[3] in Mercia and the Danelagh, and was nearly as much under monkish influence as Edward the Confessor himself. Since the Conquest many of the family have served in the Church as abbot, prebendary, dean, archdeacon, rector or vicar, but most of them will appear in the modern history of the family. The influence and support of the Church has never been neglected since the days of Herewald, Bishop of Sherborne.

[1] Leofric and Algar are both names of Old Norse or Scandinavian origin, and at the end of the eighth century Norse and Danish families had settled in the country of the Lindiswaras, with whom the ancestors of Hereward had intermarried. Lincoln was always the chief town of the five great cities of the Danelagh. The last Earl Algar, in the reign of Edward the Confessor, was made Earl of the entire Anglo-Danish province of East Anglia in his father's lifetime.

[2] See Palgrave (Cohen), "Proofs and Illustrations to Commonwealth."

[3] "Nobilis fundator multorum coenabiorum tempore Edwardi secundi, Ethelredi, Cnutonis, Haroldi, Hardicanuti et Edwardi tertii regum Angliæ."—Dugdale, "Monasticon."

The Danish troubles commenced shortly after the bishop's death, and the Saxons were in a great measure superseded by the Danish leaders; but the Mercian family appears to have held a middle course with Dane and Saxon, and as a matter of fact there was really not much to choose between them. The name became Harvard in Danish, and the subsequent marriage with Duke Oslac's daughter shows that the Harvards were on an equality with the leading Danish family, whose ancestress, Osburga, wife of King Ethelwulf and daughter of the cupbearer, Oslac, was progenitrix of eleven kings, of which four were sons, and seven others their lineal descendants.[1] The leading Danes became Christians and were baptized by Alfred the Great, and from the beginning of the tenth century could have differed very slightly from the Anglo-Saxons. The marriage with Duke Oslac's daughter may have contributed to raise Leofric to the Earldom of Mercia. He and Godwin were second only to the king. Leofric's son, Alfgar, was made Earl of East Anglia during his father's lifetime, and Alfgar's sons, Edwin and Morcar, were made respectively Earls of Warwick and Northumberland. Hereward would no doubt have been ennobled had he not excited the jealousy of Earl Godwin's sons, and forfeited the goodwill of the ascetic and narrow-minded King, by some boyish escapade savouring more of Saxon roughness than Norman polish, for which the lad was expatriated; and after a short tour in Northumbria, Cornwall, and Ireland, he settled in Ghent or other towns in the Low Countries until 1067.

His career in Flanders will be discussed hereafter. The next chapter will refer to Hereward's early life, his boyish character and troubles, his banishment from England, his first love and happy marriage with the Lady Torfrida.

With scant material, and the dull cold light of musty chronicles, supplemented by perverted history, it is hard indeed to produce a breathing picture, or harmonious sketch. In the absence of reliable information, to clothe an imperfect

[1] Ethelbald, Ethelbert, Ethelred I., Alfred the Great, Edward the Elder, Edwy, Edgar, Edward the Martyr, Ethelred II., Edmund Ironside, Edward the Confessor.

skeleton of fact with a living form of truth is a difficult matter, without trenching upon the region of romance and imagination to an extent irreconcilable with the object of this sketch. It would have been so much pleasanter to elaborate the story with pages of bright fiction. But the flowery meads of word-painting and the warm light of colour must yield to beaten paths and staid monotone.

We have to plod on with dry matter of fact, and to work over disputed ground almost every inch of the way ; but in our dreary pilgrimage to long forgotten shrines we shall recall incidents worthy of a place in the finest romances of English chivalry or history.

Chapter iij.

Hereward: His Early History, Banishment and Marriage.

> " Of his stature he was of even lengthe,
> And wonderly deliver and grete of strengthe:
> And he had be sometime in Chevachie,
> In Flandres, in Artois, and in Picardie,
> And borne him well, as of so litel space,
> In hope to stonden in hys ladies grace."
>   CHAUCER—*Canterbury Tales.*
>
> " Right faithful, true he was in deeds and word;
> But of his cheere did seem too solemn sad,
> Yet nothing did he dread but ever was ydrad."
>   SPENSER—*Faerie Queen*, Bk. i., canto i., st. 2.

IVIDING the personal narrative of Hereward into three tableaux, we at once enter upon particulars of his birth and parentage; and here on the very threshold of his history we find conflicting authorities. One writer declares that " Herewardus vir strenuissimus," used by Florence of Worcester, is "our whole authentic description of him." The fact is, that from the eleventh century to the present day timid writers and hostile influences have been careful to enshroud the entity of Hereward in a cloudy mist, to serve as a foil to the successful Norman victor and his descendants. From Professor Freeman we might have expected deeper research, more impartiality and juster sympathy with the Saxon people of England at the

Early History.

time of the Norman Conquest, instead of a mere fulsome glorification of the Conqueror. At that time, notwithstanding the repeated massacres of the defenceless peasantry by the lawless robber chiefs of William, the population must have numbered one hundred of Saxon birth to one Norman.

Professor Freeman, besides what he calls his only reliable sources of information[1] of that period, acknowledges the importance of the Domesday record; yet he never tries to draw any practical inference from the entries respecting Hereward in connection with the Earl of Mercia's family, Alfgar, Edwin, Morcar and others. Very obscure light, or impartial opinion of Hereward, can be obtained from the latest History of the Norman Conquest.

Modern romances afford little trace of patient investigation, and it is only by the clues afforded by the ancient chronicles, the facts of Domesday, the researches of works like the "Monasticon," or archæological investigation, that any rational exposition of Hereward's history can be educed [2]

Hereward's descent from Leofric, Earl of Mercia, is sometimes discredited on account of the alleged weakness of cotemporary proof; but on the other hand the Domesday records show distinctly that the same lands were held at various times by Hereward, Alfgar, Edwin, and Morcar, and although this may only be a coincidence, it is so remarkable that while in one instance it would afford presumptive evidence of inheritance and relationship, in its combined effect it affords corroborative proof of Hereward's descent from Leofric, Earl of Mercia. It was a difficult matter to alienate real estate at that time and for long after the Norman Conquest. Even if forfeited for treason or felony, it was generally restored to the next heir of the same family, whence arose the old legal doggerel axiom,

"The father to the bough,
The son to the plough";

---

[1] Florence Wig., the Saxon Chronicle and Orderic Vit.
[2] The details of Miss C. Yonge's "Cameos from English History" are inaccurate. The Rev. Charles Kingsley's "Hereward the Wake" could not be accepted as an authority by a schoolboy, and was written with the obvious purpose of manufacturing a noble lineage for personal friends named "Wake."

implying that after the father's execution the estate should be restored to the son.

The generally accepted account is that Hereward's father was Leofric, Lord of Bourne in Lincolnshire. Was this Leofric the Earl of Mercia? Incontestable Domesday records the former owner of Bourne as Morcar,[1] who possibly held it during Hereward's absence in Flanders. One writer says Hereward's estate in Lincolnshire was at Locton and not at Bourne; but the family probably had several residences in East Anglia, and Bourne was undoubtedly one of them, as it descended to Hereward's daughter Torfrida and her husband, Hugh de Evermue, a Norman. At the time of the Domesday Survey the land at Bourne had been conferred upon Oger the Breton. Now this man had obtained some other of Hereward's estates, and it is therefore most probable that he obtained Bourne by a trick, contending that it was Morcar's property forfeited by his rebellion. Hereward evidently refused to surrender his rights, and after his forces in the fens of Ely were scattered, he retired to the woods of Bourne, until he made his peace with William; and according to Ingulph, Bourne became the property of his daughter Torfrida, who had married Hugh de Evermue. The testimony of Ingulph is in many respects of value, although doubt has been cast upon it. Even Freeman says, "The story of the false Ingulph (pp. 67, 70) is not to be wholly cast aside, as it may contain genuine Croyland traditions." It is from this authority we get the alleged parentage from Leofric of Brunne or Bourne. Moreover, this Leofric was "cognatus illius magni comitis Herfordensis Radini, qui Godam Edwardi regis sororem duxerat in uxorem."

This passage affords a most important link in the Hereward pedigree, as Ralph the timid, Earl of Hereford,[2] although

[1] The Morkery Woods at Bourne still exist, and in their venerable sylvan antiquity commemorate the primæval days of England, when the aged oaks still bore the mistletoe sacred in Pagan Druidical rites and the worship of Baal; while the grandly-spreading yew trees, planted by no hand of man, still show signs of the demand made upon them by English archers, whose stout bows and stouter hearts maintained the honour of their country in the battlefields of Europe.

[2] This title had been borne by Leofric in the time of Edward II. and Ethelred.

nephew, and not brother-in-law of King Edward, gave kinship to his relatives Leofric and Hereward to the King himself.[1]

Besides the connection shown between Hereward and Morcar in the lands at Bourne, we find in Domesday that Gilbert of Ghent held (Ladbroc) Ladbroke, in Warwickshire, from Turchil, and it is distinctly stated that it formerly belonged to Edwin, and that Hereward had it. It was, in fact, one of the estates returned to Hereward when he made peace with the King. It was natural that after the death of Alfgar, Edwin and Morcar should have taken care of Hereward's lands whilst he was in exile. Again it is stated that Merston Jabet, another estate returned to Hereward, formerly belonged to Alfgar. It would show a disregard of all evidence to hold these successive incidents as mere coincidence, or anything less than strong corroborative proof of kinship.

Without attaching undue importance to the fact, we must hold, with the support of this evidence, that Leofric, Earl of Mercia was Lord of Bourne and father of Hereward, this opinion coinciding with that of Sir Henry Ellis[2] and Mr. T. Wright. There is, moreover, other important collateral evidence that Hereward was of noble descent. His mother, Leofric's wife, said to be a daughter of Thorold, Sheriff of Lincolnshire, was related to the noble house of Oslac, which from the days of Ethelwulf has borne a race of kings to England down to the Confessor, and Oslac in the time of Edgar was probably the most powerful noble outside the reigning house.

---

[1] Henry, Earl of Surrey, was beheaded by Henry VIII. for using the arms of Edward the Confessor on the fictitious claim that Howards and Herewards were one, and the latter being of the royal blood of Edward, the Howards were entitled to bear the royal arms. The most important charge of treason against him is King Henry VIII.'s statement that "his ancestors never bare, nor he of right ought to bear" the arms of Edward the Confessor, of which he was found guilty, sentenced and executed.

[2] In his Introduction to Domesday Book, vol. i., p. 308, he refers to Hereward as "the mirror of Knighthood in the Saxon period." Referring to MS. Harl., 447, he says: "This was Hereward, or Herward, the younger son of Leofric, Earl of Mercia, who was chosen by the prelates and nobility, who retired to the Isle of Ely after the Conqueror's invasion, to be the general of their forces."

The description of Hereward in the Chronicle betokens noble origin and high status,

> "Un des meilleurs del region."
> *Chron. Ang. Norm. Geoff. Gaimar.*

He is also recorded as godson to the noble Gilbert, Lord of Ghent, one of the richest men in England, related to Count Baldwin of Flanders, and representative of the diplomatic interests and important commercial guilds of Flanders in England, holding immense estates in fourteen English counties. The trade of London and York was then largely maintained by the Flemings. Another of Hereward's Warwickshire estates was at Coleshill, contiguous to Kingsbury Hall, the ancient residence of the Saxon kings, which afterwards descended with many other manors to Hereward's mother. Archæologists have discovered the remains of a house or castle at Coleshill, which may have been Hereward's abode. The royal castle of Tamworth, where King Edward resided, was not far away.

That he was eventually made chief of the English at Ely is the natural corollary of all this overwhelming evidence. His bravery alone would not have sufficed to outweigh the claims of nobles like Morcar. Hereward showed the utmost contempt for the mushroom Norman chiefs, such as Ivo de Taillebois, the Warrennes, William and Frederic, Thorold, Abbot of Peterborough, and the whole of the new proprietors in the nine counties adjacent to Ely, all of whom he harried, took prisoners and ransomed, or killed in combat; and his bearing throughout the war and in his negotiations for peace was characterized by true nobility. He was never vanquished. As long as there was hope, he threw away the scabbard, and offered his life and fortunes on the altar of his country with complete self-abnegation. He fought for hearth and home when all but his personal retainers deserted the patriotic cause, and he even won the esteem of William, who granted him amnesty on most honourable terms.

The exact date of Hereward's birth can only be surmised. At the camp of Ely he was married, and in the full flower of manhood, probably thirty-two to thirty-six years of age. Assuming his birth in 1032, he was thirty-five years of age at

Early History.

Ely in 1067. Leofric III., described in the "Monasticon" as the noble founder of many abbeys, in the time of Edward II., Ethelred, Canute, Harold, Hardicanute, and Edward the Confessor, begat Alfgar, afterwards Earl, and is buried at Coventry. He lived from 975 to 1057. His father was Leofwine, Earl of Lincoln. Leofric was made Earl of Hereford, Chester, and, in the time of Canute, about 1017, Earl of Mercia. The confidence and favour of Canute were no doubt largely due to the alliance of the Saxon Earl by marriage with the Danish family of Oslac. In 1041, Edward the Confessor restored the Saxon line, but having spent twenty-seven years at the Norman Court was surrounded by Norman favourites who absorbed the chief offices of State; and under these adverse influences young Hereward, a Saxon of the Saxons, despising the French language and fashions adopted at the English Court, was accused of roughness to the young Frenchmen and expatriated.

Of Hereward's early training we can only gather, from the customs of the time, that he received the instruction necessary for a youth intended to bear arms;[1] and no doubt exists that he became highly accomplished in these exercises. His physique was well developed, and he showed great strength of body and mind. His feelings against the Norman usurpers were aggravated by his early quarrels, and subsequent Norman insults offered to his mother at Bourne. That his character was impetuous and daring beyond measure we have ample proof, but there is no indication of weakness of character, malice, recklessness, or folly in any of his hair-breadth risks and schemes. He understood the art of soldiering better than the flower of the Norman army, and his character stands out in high contrast from the Normans, who were rapacious, prodigal, debauched, and cruel, without any redeeming feature. A certain savage sense of justice distinguished the Norman King William in his best days; but in the decline of life his evil characteristics were accentuated by atrocious murders[2] and cruelty to the vanquished race far worse than death.

[1] See Appendix: "Hereward as Esquire."
[2] That of Waltheof, Earl of Northumberland, amongst others. See Appendix: "Atrocious cruelty of William I."

Hereward's high spirit and English breeding must have prevented his finding favour with such a connection as King Edward. The Confessor is described as being "of a cold and unsympathetic nature, with the habits of devotion and the observances of the cloister. His piety, however sincere, was sheer monkery of the lowest type, and he has been accused of actual cruelty to his own relations."[1] Leofric, Earl of Mercia, was second only to the King in austerity and discipline, whilst Hereward's character more resembled that of Alfgar and the sons of Godwin. During his lifetime St. Edward was looked upon by his people as an ascetic. It was not until his death he was made much of by the priests, his beneficiaries, and canonized by the Pope. Young Hereward no doubt rebelled against the restraint and priestly counsel imposed upon him, and was led by his natural temperament to prefer exercises of arms, and the sports of the field, to the discipline of a monastic life.

There is not a shadow of evidence to indicate that Hereward ever robbed a servant of the Church, as stated by Kingsley, whose utter disregard of facts will be referred to in a subsequent chapter.[2] He was certainly expatriated, but without any sentence of outlawry, which would have entailed the forfeiture of his estates.[3] Moreover, so far as the records

---

[1] "Universal History," vol. ii., p. 197 ; Cassell and Co.

[2] See Chapter VII. and Appendix.

[3] An outlaw has always been a felon by the common law of England, and his lands held liable to forfeiture. See Cromwell's Institutes of Peace, folio 151. His protection and privileges under Frank-Law were forfeited, and "*his lands, goods, and chattels are to be seized unto the King's hands*, and *his lands must be estreaped* (escheated), *his trees rooted up, and his body committed to prison.*"

By the laws of King Edward the Confessor, a Saxon who refused to submit himself to justice was in a condition of "woolferthfod." If he could then be taken alive he was brought before the King, and if he, in fear of apprehension, defended himself, he might be slain, and his head brought unto the King, for he carried a wolf's head—that is to say, his head was no more to be accounted of than a wolf's head. See laws of King Edward the Confessor, by Master Lambert, folio 127, No. 7, and Brac., lib. iii., tract 2, cap. ii. This is written "wuluesheaued" by Roger Honedean, part. poster Annal., folio 343.

The records of Domesday show that Hereward's lands were not confiscated, and therefore a necessary part of the sentence of outlawry had never been carried out.

Banishment.   23

afford a clue, Hereward's case was not brought before the Witan in the usual manner, but was dealt with solely by the King, at the instance of Hereward's father, Leofric. Here again, we have corroboration of the belief that Hereward's father was Earl of Mercia. If he had been an ordinary thane the King would not have interfered with the ordinary course of law.

The exact nature and degree of Hereward's offence can only be conjectured from the surrounding facts. The son of a nobleman, he was often at Court, if indeed he was not brought up in Edward's household. He was about twenty years of age when he was sent abroad, and his youth is still more apparent from the fact that he was guided by his godfather, Gilbert of Ghent, in all his movements.

Whether at Court or with his father, Hereward was being trained for the profession of arms, according to the custom of the time, as page, esquire, and knight. The King was surrounded by effeminate youths who had accompanied him from France, and there could have been little friendship between these fops and the sturdy young Saxon. They probably excelled in dancing, playing on the harp, and in the meaner offices of the household, while Hereward was distinguished in field sports, and the pastimes of wrestling, tilting with spears, etc. Amongst other exercises an esquire was taught to vault on a horse in complete armour,[1] to scale walls, and spring over ditches with the same encumbrance. To these athletic feats Hereward appears to have added the device of throwing one of the French pages on the low roof of a Saxon house, and letting him roll off, and it is more than probable that he played with the quarterstaff and tilted with a blunt spear in a too earnest fashion to be agreeable to his less manly companions. His Saxon comrades would hardly have objected to a little rough play at times.

Such a poor creature as King Edward the Confessor could

From all the accounts extant, his offence was simply a boyish escapade in tumbling about some of the effeminate youths at Court, who had probably been brought up with the King in France, and complained to him of the prowess of young Hereward in cowardly and un-English style.

[1] Mill's "History of the Crusades," Note F.

find little sympathy for a youth who openly showed a distaste for religious austerities, and seldom observed the fasts and festivals of the Church. The hostility of the sons of Godwin, his father's rival, was also in his disfavour at Court; and although there is no reason to believe that Hereward was guilty of any offence beyond a mere boyish escapade, King Edward, at the instance of his father, and under the guiding hand of Providence, passed upon him a sentence of banishment.

It is impossible to disconnect this fact from the previous expatriation of Earl Alfgar, the eldest son of the Earl of Mercia, which was brought about by the intrigues of Godwin and his sons, and there is, therefore, strong reason to believe that it was the desire of Harold and his brothers to secure the dismissal from court of both Leofric's sons in order to prevent any favour being shown to them in the matter of the succession to the crown, for there was undoubted relationship between Edward and Leofric. On this account only is it easy to understand why so severe a punishment was inflicted for a venial offence.

The punishment awarded was very different from outlawry, which would necessarily have involved forfeiture, and the proceedings would have been conducted before the Witan which had the power to inflict it. The procedure adopted by the King was no doubt in accordance with a precedent in the reign of Æthelstan. The Witan of Kent having found that even with earl and bishop it was powerless to deal with offenders of the highest rank, prayed King Æthelstan: "That if any man be so rich or of so great kin that he cannot be punished, or will not cease from his wrong doing, you may settle how he may be carried away into some other part of your kingdom, be the case whom he may, villein or thane."[1] Such appears to have been the course adopted in Hereward's case, and he was sent to travel in foreign countries for an indefinite period, the result of a Court intrigue, and undue influence upon the mind of an ascetic, worn out by continued austerities, and abstraction from the active business of life.

In 1052 Alfgar was banished or driven out of the kingdom

[1] Thorpe, "Ancient Laws," i., 217.

Banishment. 25

by Harold's influence, and a few years afterwards Hereward was also driven away. The young chief's first intention was to join Malcolm Canmore, then struggling with Macbeth for the crown of Scotland, with the design of invoking his aid against Harold's brother Tostig, recently appointed Earl of Northumberland, but his godfather, Gilbert, Lord of Ghent, related to Earl Baldwin of Flanders, who resided at York, hearing of his plan, sent for him and persuaded him not to disturb the peace of that part of the country.[1]

Acting under the advice of his godfather, Gilbert of Ghent, he appears to have given up his trip to the north, and travelled to Ireland, where the chiefs entertained a most favourable opinion of King Edward, so much so that Richard II. used the arms of Edward in Ireland instead of the leopards of Normandy.[2] There are no details of this visit, or of a tour subsequently made to Cornwall, but he appears to have been well received, and to have returned uninjured. In the meantime introductions and necessary funds, sent from Bourne, or provided by his pattern godfather, prepared the way for his trip to Flanders. His subsequent marriage to a Flemish lady of rank and position shows that he was duly accredited, and his renown in arms, strengthened by his prowess in any expeditions he may have joined against the enemies of the Earl of Flanders, recommended him to the regard of the lady. Outlaws are not usually welcomed abroad, but Hereward must have had strong personal re-

---

[1] "Quod ubi quidam Gisebritus de Gant comperit scilicet expulsionem ejus pro illo misit. Filiosus enim erat divitis illius. Et profectus ultra Northumberland ad eum pervenit."

[2] Froissart relates that all the kings of Ireland were friendly to Edward and his people. When Richard II. went to Ireland in 1395, he found that "Edward the Confessor was more respected and feared than any sovereign of England before or since." So he left off bearing the arms of England, "the libards and fleur-de-lises quarterly," and bare the arms of St. Edward—that is, "A cross patent gold and goules, with four white martinets in the field." The lions, or, more correctly, the "libards," had been introduced from Normandy, and were not the ancient arms of England. At Senlac the Norman device, as shown in the Bayeux tapestry, was a cross and a dragon. The dragon was the bearing of the Cymrians, and was adopted at an early period by the Saxons of Wessex. Harold bore on his shield a cross and tigers' heads. The origin of the lions, or "libards," is very obscure.

4

commendations, besides the influence of his godfather, to ensure such an agreeable issue to his troubles. He appears, in fact, to have been borne along upon the flood of Fortune's tide, and to have fully realized the old adage, " Fortes fortuna juvat."

It hardly admits of doubt that his interview with the Sieur Gilbert of Ghent, his godfather, in Northumberland, had a very important bearing on Hereward's future career. His journey to Flanders and his subsequent proceedings must have been largely influenced by the advice and assistance of his kind godfather. Gilbert's position in England was that of a nobleman of great wealth and influence,[1] and related to Baldwin, Count of Flanders, he was probably the lord and chief man in Ghent. Bruges, not far from Ghent, was the principal residence of the Counts of Flanders, the fortress or castle of Lille being their chief stronghold of defence, while they had a country residence at Marle, two miles from Bruges.

Gilbert must have been an intimate friend of Hereward's family, as his son afterwards married the grand-daughter and sole heiress of Lucia, sister of Hereward, and thereby he succeeded by right of his wife to the Earldom of Lincoln. We may therefore rest assured that Hereward had the full benefit of this friendship, and that Gilbert's kinsmen and connections in Bruges and Ghent received Hereward most cordially. He was probably lodged in one of Gilbert's houses, and became acquainted with the Flemish nobles and leading burgesses, and about this period of his history he came under the notice of the fair lady Torfrida, who subsequently became his wife.

At this time, also, his love of arms and the sports of chivalry met with encouragement from the martial spirit of the Flemish people. The Flemings were hard men, and whether as artisans, traders, or men-at-arms, they held their own with credit amongst the nations of that day. They also maintained a character for bravery and independence conspicuous amongst all the tribes of Germany, and in such a school Hereward's military training must have been completed

[1] See the account of his large estates in fourteen counties shown in Domesday Book.

under the most favourable conditions, and his martial ardour and lofty spirit stimulated by surrounding influences.

The English chronicles, however, afford little guide as to Hereward's life in Flanders, but fair inferences may be deduced from the known facts. Whether he attached himself to Count Baldwin, or to his son Robert, or to the Count of Guisnes, we may only learn at some future time, when Flemish records hitherto unknown may enlighten us.

The particulars of his alleged shipwreck on landing in Flanders appear only as a visionary outline, and certainly the chief fact in connection with his landing, whether shipwrecked or not, is centred in the undoubtedly cordial reception he met with, and the congenial pursuits in which he became occupied. In tournaments and knightly exercises, who more skilful than Hereward? In feats of strength, who bore off the palm? If hard blows were exchanged, who more ready than Hereward to receive and pay back with interest? He is described by Florence of Worcester as " vir strenuissimus," which seems to include besides strength and vigour, energy of body and mind, patience, perseverance and endurance, as well as unflinching resolution, indomitable courage, capability of resource in conception, and tenacity of purpose in execution.

If the adjective "strenuissimus " is allowed to bear most or all of the meanings here assigned to it, it is by no means impossible to form a fair ideal presentment of the Saxon hero as he stood in his lifetime, with actively working mind, his eyes bright with intelligence and resource for every emergency. No thought for danger troubled his smooth brow. His features must have indicated the character of the man, and if there is any truth in physiognomy he must have borne a well-formed mouth of decided character, a straight or Saxon nose, and a full chin somewhat projecting, while the jaw, square and massive, gave determination to the lower part of the face, and the well developed head and moderately high forehead indicated his mental capacity and ready wit, not only in deeds of arms and in overcoming difficulties, but in the subtle military arts of stratagem and surprise, of personal self-control, and complete self-sacrifice on emergency, as over and over again he risked himself in the power of his enemies, when reconnoitring their camp or testing their resources.

Various commentators more or less accurate have described Hereward's physical characteristics at some length, and from these qualifications, which must reasonably have been inherent in a "vir strenuissimus," we may realize his form in outline and development, allowing due roughness of exterior to meet the conditions of a race not over-civilized, and more remarkable then as now for bluntness of manner and plainness of speech and dress, than for French fopperies or superficial effeminacy.

Accounts of the great personal strength of Hereward record the fact that he was enabled to overcome his enemies in combat by simply throwing himself upon them, without resort to sword or battle-axe. With the latter weapon he must have been as much dreaded as the lion-hearted Richard. It is further stated that he was so skilled in the use of his weapons, from bow and arrow to lance and sword, that he was not excelled by any of his contemporaries. He was an excellent horseman, and equally skilful when fighting on foot. During the time he harried the Normans in nine adjacent counties, it was usual to march thirty or forty miles in the night, and at daybreak, by a skilful attack upon the Norman outpost or castle, to scatter its defenders, to take prisoners the chiefs and their families, and to hold them to ransom. But within twenty-four hours Hereward was back at his own fastness in the woods of Bourne, still called the Morkery Woods, where he defied attack or pursuit.

Hereward was essentially a leader of men, originating and arranging his plans without aid from anyone, and placing himself in front of his men, he claimed as his right, and as a matter of course, the post of danger and responsibility.

As King Alfred had done at the time of the Danish invasion under Guthrum, Hereward took upon himself to reconnoitre the enemy's camp in disguise, and penetrated the heart of the Norman position at Ely.

His moral worth was no less remarkable than his distinguished prowess as a military leader. One writer only has ventured to ascribe baseness to him with especial reference to his combat with Frederick Warrenne. This is the writer of

Marriage.

the "de Hydâ,"[1] considered a competent authority by Freeman, but without doubt a Norman scribe, who looked upon all Saxons as rebels and criminals, and their resistance to Norman atrocities as baseness of the lowest order. This may account for his language towards Hereward, who, he alleges, killed Frederick Warrenne "amongst his other wickednesses." All other writers have combined to praise him. Sir H. Ellis, in his "Introduction to Domesday," refers to him as "the mirror of knighthood," and if Florence of Worcester had agreed with the "de Hydâ," he would probably have used "sceleratissimus" as a more appropriate epithet than "strenuissimus." As a matter of fact, there has never been a suspicion of baseness or bad faith in his stormy and chequered career, and the statement in "de Hydâ" must be taken at its value. Even the Norman writers of the Saxon Chronicle, and subsequent to the Conquest, give Hereward full credit for all knightly prowess, and utter no word to his disadvantage.

From the time when he was brought into contact with the effeminate French youths at the English Court, and was placed under monastic discipline, it is clear to all who study character that his soul revolted against his companions and spiritual masters.

As we have sketched his features, let us add, a figure of moderate height, thick-set and muscular, an arm that could fell an ox, but the frame generally light and elastic, with no superfluous flesh, great strength of loin and back, framework well proportioned, hands and feet of moderate size, but the ankles and wrists wonderfully elastic and supple. Such a figure, roughly as it is sketched, in the absence of a better may be taken as a counterfeit presentment of Hereward the "vir strenuissimus" of England at the time of the Norman Conquest.

Leaving the young esquire to qualify himself for his future knighthood, we must endeavour to acquire some knowledge of the lady Torfrida. She appears to have held a conspicuous place in the Court of Bruges. Clever and beautiful, with a good fortune at her disposal, she appears to have smiled upon

[1] A chronicle written by the monks at the monastery or abbey of Hyde.

Hereward even before he was aware of the happiness in store for him. Torfrida is described as a young lady noble and beautiful, devoted to the liberal sciences, and equally skilled in the mechanical arts.[1] The chronicle also expatiates upon her womanly softness and sound judgment, and if there had not been tough work preparing in his native land, the episode of his marriage would have suited the climax of a novel, and he would have lived happy ever afterwards. But stirring times were at hand. News of the contemplated Norman invasion must have reached Flanders before it was known in England. Hereward's attitude at this time can only be understood by his desire to withhold support from Harold, the son of his father's enemy, Earl Godwin, and his indifference towards the Duke of Normandy. In any case, he preferred to bide his time.

It cannot be doubted that Hereward showed sound judgment in abstaining from the first conflict between Harold and William of Normandy. The enmity which had long existed between the houses of Leofric and Godwin was by no means set at rest when Harold assumed the crown of England; and there was even less reason why Hereward should support the Norman invader. The most determined of England's patriots would be the last to assist a hostile claimant to the Saxon throne of England, and he deemed it wisest to watch the course of events before deciding upon a particular line of action. He probably anticipated the defeat of William's army of freebooters, impelled neither by love of country nor a sense of justice. Each man fought for his own hand, and the sole object of the war to William's supporters was the plunder of England, which remarkably good luck, under the will of Providence, enabled them to obtain.

In subsequent times, during the Civil Wars of the Roses and the unhappy events in the Stuart dynasty, the Herewards, feeling that both sides were in the wrong, refused to sacrifice themselves for either party, rightly judging that the more the quarrel was promoted, the greater the loss and disadvantage to the people of England.

[1] "Puella nobilis et pulchra, scientiæ liberalitatis multum dedita, in mechanicâque arte etiam peritissima."

Marriage.

News travelled slowly in the eleventh century, and it was not until Hereward obtained confirmation of the reports of spoliation and rapine on the part of the Norman victors that he hastened back to England. At that time the Saxon estates were being parcelled out amongst the Norman chiefs, and the Saxon people suffered every kind of indignity. Hereward's home at Bourne had been assailed by a Norman chief, who obtained temporary possession of it, ill-treating his mother and her dependents. He returned to Bourne with a chosen band of followers—Ibe Winter,[1] his brother-in-arms; Eghelric, his cousin; Ital, Alfric, Seawald, and many others. Having communicated with his old friends in Lincolnshire, he raised a small band of men-at-arms, and before his return was generally known, he surprised the Normans at Bourne enjoying a banquet in his own hall. According to their custom, they were highly jocose, caricaturing the Saxon methods of singing and dancing. A change must indeed have come over the spirit of their dream, when Hereward and his faithful followers burst into the house and cut down the revellers with their battle-axes, scarcely allowing one solitary fugitive to carry the news to Ivo de Taillebois at Spalding.

Having restored his mother, the widow of Earl Leofric, to her home, and leaving a sufficient guard to protect her, he returned to Flanders to reassure his wife and bring her to England, feeling assured that the time had now arrived when the presence of every Englishman would be required to resist the fearful oppression of the Norman adventurers. It cannot be gainsaid that Hereward was strictly within his rights in resisting force by force. William had outlawed himself, inasmuch as he had sworn at his coronation, according to the oath of St. Dunstan, to execute justice and to govern England *according to the laws of Alfred and Edward.* It is certain he never had any intention to observe this most sacred oath. The only form of government with which he had any acquaintance was the feudal system as administered on the Continent, which differed in every respect from the Saxon laws. He had promised a large share of plunder and the landed pro-

[1] Robert Hereward, of Aldeburgh, succeeded to the estate of Bultees, also called Herewards, from Ino. Winter, about A.D. 1350.

prietorship to his followers before he set sail from Normandy.[1] No Danish viking or Pict cattle-lifter committed such cruel atrocities or wholesale robbery as this unscrupulous Norman barbarian, and having broken his oath to the people, he was no longer entitled to any respect but that given and taken by the sword. Hereward was never an aggressor. He defended his property and people, and punished intruders. Only, after every hope of justice had died away, he exacted retribution from the Norman criminals, and allowed none to escape his avenging arm. There has never been a word said against the justice of his cause, or of the means adopted by him to strike a heavy blow at the Normans in return for their slaughter and plunder of the unoffending and helpless Saxon peasantry.

The scene now changes to the Camp of Refuge in the fens of Ely, and the brilliant exploits of Hereward in his campaign against William and the whole strength of the Norman army.

[1] See Appendix: "Belamonte, Earl of Mellent."

Chapter iv.

Hereward: the Camp of Refuge.

> "Des utlaghes mulz i avait
> Uns gentil hom leur sire estait,
> Ki Hereward avait a nun
> Un des meilleurs del region."
>   GEOFF. GAIMAR—*Chron. Ang. Norm.*

> "Many outlaws were collected;
> A gentleman, their lord, directed;
> For Hereward, second to none,
> Was noblest in that region."

THE Battle of Hastings took place on October 14, 1066. William was crowned on Christmas Day; and although the chief Saxon estates were at once apportioned amongst the Normans, it was not until William went to Normandy in July, 1067, that the reign of cruelty, and extermination of the Saxons, became universal. Before the end of this year Hereward returned from Flanders and recovered his estates from the retainers of Ivo de Taillebois.

His second return home, accompanied by his wife Torfrida, was probably in the autumn of 1067, when the full magnitude of the undertaking in which he had engaged was realized. His first step was to place his wife in safety in one of the religious houses—but whether Croyland, Peterborough, or Coventry, is not known. She was probably accompanied by Hereward's mother, and all her female dependents. During

1067-1068 he appears to have been chiefly occupied in establishing a Camp of Refuge in the Isle of Ely, where the homeless peasantry obtained asylum; in preventing the Normans from holding possession of the estates of which they had despoiled the Saxon proprietors, and in retaliating upon them for their cruel treatment of the peasants. Ivo de Taillebois was an especial object of hatred. His name indicates his humble calling as wood tollman in Anjou, and in England his conduct was that of a parvenu. He was pompous and insolent;[1] his vassals knelt to receive his orders, and he and his men amused themselves by tormenting the poorer Saxons. He set his dogs at them and their flocks, lamed and drowned their cattle, and killed their poultry. He even harassed the monks and plundered the Spalding cell of the great Abbey at Croyland, and Abbot Ingulph, who had been William's secretary, could obtain no redress. Like master, like man. Hereward, however, gave him no peace, and when the Camp of Refuge at Ely was broken up, took him prisoner, and held Taillebois as hostage while he made his peace with William, who had then established his authority as King, and against whom further resistance was useless.

On his first return from Flanders, he was knighted by his uncle, Brand, Abbot of Peterborough, and his first act was to challenge[2] Frederick de Warrenne, brother of William

[1] Miss Charlotte Yonge's "Cameos of English History," vol. i.

[2] "The most common mode of determining the merits both of civil action and criminal processes was the trial by battle.* The origin of this mode of decision was coeval with the rudest beginnings of society, when all considerations were personal, and revenge was the object of punishment.

"Among military nations the trial by battle prevailed over the ordeal, and other appeals to heavenly interposition. The causes which were to be tried by battle, and which could not be decided by the court without it, were murder, treason, apparent homicides . . . and all other things which concerned life, members, and right honour."

Certain ceremonies and procedure in law were laid down before the duel could be fought. The combat took place between six and nine o'clock, in the presence of the feudal lord. If one called for mercy, or was slain, in either case the punishment of hanging was inflicted. In Hereward's combat with Frederick de Warrenne, it is doubtful whether all these ceremonies were observed. The duel was probably a "combat à l'outrance" between armed

* From Mill's "History of the Crusades," vol. i., chapter viii., p. 329.

Warrenne, the King's son-in-law, who had been one of the chief assailants of his home at Bourne, to mortal combat, according to the "wager of battle." Frederick refused to acknowledge his knighthood as having been conferred by a spiritual lord,[1] and the other Norman chiefs agreed with him. Hereward went to Lynn and compelled Frederick, in spite of his retainers, to come out of the house, and slew him in the combat.

His next adventure was with Thorold, lately Abbot of Malmesbury. William heard he was always fighting with the English monks, and that he kept a large body of men-at-arms to enforce his orders. The King said: "I'll find him his match! He shall go to Peterborough, where Hereward will give him enough fighting."[2] He was therefore transferred to Peterborough, where the monks, dreading his rapacity, appealed to Hereward for aid. He, with the full concurrence of the monks, carried off all the treasures of the Abbey to the fens of Ely, where, since 1067, he had begun to establish a camp of refuge. Soon after Thorold arrived at Peterborough attended by one hundred and sixty men-at-arms, and at once united his forces with Ivo de Taillebois against Hereward. The latter by a ruse drew off Taillebois' men, and captured Thorold, who had to pay thirty-six thousand marcs[3] for his own ransom and that of the Church property. Hereward now established himself permanently in the fens with his two nephews, Siward the Red and Siward the White, his own personal following, and a considerable number of Saxon thanes, freemen, and peasants. The largest number of men present at any time with Hereward was under four thousand, of whom one thousand were killed at the capture of the camp. At first

---

knights mounted, with spear, battle-axe, and dagger, or on foot with sword and dagger, and the esquires and friends of each party the only witnesses.

[1] William Rufus was afterwards knighted by Archbishop Lanfranc.

[2] "Cameos of English History," by Miss C. Yonge.

[3] About £20,000 of our money. Not an extravagant sum, when it is considered that the monasteries absorbed nearly all the wealth of the country, and the princes of the Church had often more wealth at their disposal than the secular lords. The monastery of St. Denis redeemed its Abbot from captivity with six hundred and eighty-five pounds of gold, about £25,000. This was at the time of the siege of Paris by the Danes, A.D. 885.

their headquarters were at the monastery, where monks and warriors sat side by side in the refectory, the walls and roof being equipped like an armoury with every description of weapon and armour, so that the comrades, lay and spiritual, should be prepared for any sudden call to arms. Here he was joined by all those who had been dispossessed of their lands, and who for not surrendering themselves to Norman violence were called outlaws; here also resorted the most daring spirits of England, and the ancestors of those who at the present day hold bravery and freedom as inseparable.

> "Chevaliers en ce monde cy
> Ne peuvent vivre sans soucy:
> Ils doivent le peuple defendre,
> Et leur sang pour le foy espandre."
> *Song of the Crusades.*

Edwin and Morcar left William's Court while he was absent in Normandy in 1067 and 1068, and visited the camp at Ely, when it was agreed with Hereward that he should command the men at Ely, Morcar joining him, while Edwin should endeavour to assemble an army in the north with the aid of Malcolm, King of Scotland. But treachery dogged his footsteps, and although he took the coast route, three of his followers, brothers in blood, as in treason, agreed to lead him into an ambush of Norman troops. He fought bravely, but was killed at the head of twenty horsemen who were with him. The traitors, on taking his head to William, were themselves banished the kingdom.

Edwin, except as a noble of the highest rank, cannot be considered a great loss to the cause at Ely, where the camp was being rapidly increased, and Hereward was constructing a castle of wood, as a citadel for the camp, which the peasantry for many years afterwards called Hereward's Castle.

A gloomy and unattractive picture of the fen country is given by Crabbe, the Suffolk poet:

> "On either side
> Is level fen, a prospect wild and wide,
> With dykes on either hand, by ocean's self supplied.
> Far on the right the distant sea is seen,
> And salt springs that feed the marsh between.
> Beneath an ancient bridge the straiten'd flood
> Rolls through its sloping banks of shiny mud;

> Near it a sunken boat resists the tide,
> That frets and hurries to th' opposing side.
> The rushes sharp that on the borders grow
> Bend their brown flowerets to the stream below,
> Nor hedge, nor tree, conceals the glowing sun;
> Birds, save a watery tribe, the district shun,
> Nor chirp among the reeds where bitter waters run."

Earth mounds, denoting the burial-places of forgotten Danish heroes, are plentiful along the coast, the cliffs overlooking the sea being selected as the favourite resting-place of the departed spirit of the turbulent viking.

> "Above that grave the east winds blow,
> And from the marsh-lands, drifting slow,
> The sea-fog comes, with evermore
> The wave-wash of a lonely shore,
> And seabirds melancholy cry,
> As Nature fain would typify
> The sadness of a closing scene."
>
> WHITTIER—*Lost Occasion.*

Besides the adherents of the house of Mercia, Æthelwine, Bishop of Durham, joined the camp with the men of the north, and from the distant Abbey of St. Albans, Abbot Frithric comes with his charters and a few men-at-arms, while the tenants of St. Mary of Abingdon, with a party of the men of Berks, set forth to join the champions of England.

> "Great troops of people travelled thitherward
> Both day and night, of each degree and place."

Opposed to the English were William Warrenne, Earl of Surrey, Taillebois, Count of Spalding, William Malet, whose death at Ely is recorded, and other Norman chiefs. Lastly, William himself, with his whole army, hoists his standard on the Castle of Cambridge and assumes command. He directed naval operations against the eastern part of the isle from Brandon and instituted a strict blockade. Privations the besieged had to endure, but fish and wildfowl were plentiful, and the fishermen and country folks were to a man on Hereward's side. Good store of wheat and rye, with sheep and cattle, had been driven in from the country round, and every preparation made for a protracted struggle. Hereward was the life and soul of the camp; at one time destroying the

enemies' approaches, and making sallies and inroads against the strongest posts; at another, in the disguise of a potter or a fisherman, as Alfred the Great had years before assumed that of a harper, he penetrated into the heart of William's Court, and learnt all his plans. Vainly did the besiegers try to gain a footing in the Isle of Ely, until William ordered a massive causeway to be built at Aldreth, across the Ouse. Stones, trees and hides were used in the construction, and an attack in force was made by the Normans along the causeway, but without success. Time after time the Normans were repulsed. At last a witch was placed in a wooden tower, and pushed along in front of the Norman troops, to counteract by her spells the resistance of the English. Hereward surrounded the tower, killed the guards, and burnt the witch, tower and all.

Hereward's strategy and military genius were of the highest order. Like Wellington in the lines of Torres Vedras, he adopted a strictly defensive policy in the presence of a foe superior in numbers. But when the time came for action he invariably struck a crushing blow. We see how he was ready to undertake the most difficult enterprises, and always with success. He was ever on the alert. His forethought and sagacity provided everything; not only men, and arms, and training, but food, boats, and horses were ready when required, with an unexampled stock of ready wit, energy and courage.

But, astute in forming a well-laid plan, he must have been in his element when driving back at the sword's point the flower of the Norman chivalry.

> "As when a lion sees the narrowing ring
> Of hunters, careless of the death they bring,
> He tears their darts, and bounding on their spears,
> Heeds not of wounds or death or mortal fears,
> So Hereward, who courts the hardest blows
> In thickest fight, assails his strongest foes." [1]

But the privations, severe enough to Hereward and his hardy men, were too much for the Abbot and monks of Ely;

---

[1] "Ut fera, quæ densa venantum septa coronâ
Contra tela furit, seseque haud nescia morti
Injicit, et saltu supra venabula fertur;
Haud aliter juvenis medios moriturus in hostes
Irruit, et, quà tela videt densissima, tendit."—*Æneid*, ix., 551.

moreover, William had seized upon all the abbey lands beyond the Isle of Ely. They treacherously surrendered, and showed the Normans a secret way through the marshes, and enabled them to take the Saxons by surprise and kill a thousand of them.[1] Morcar and Bishop Æthelwine also agreed to surrender, to find in lifelong fetters the reward of weakness. As to the monks, they had forty Norman men-at-arms quartered upon them for many a long year. So justice was done. Hereward retired with his personal following to the ships he had in waiting ; but he needed horses for further enterprise. He and a few followers hid under the straw in fishermen's boats, and while they were selling their wares to the Norman troops, Hereward attacked the enemy, killed some, put the rest to flight, and seized their horses.

Abandoning his position in the fens of Ely, Hereward now retired with his trusty followers to the family estate at Bourne, which had been conferred on Oger the Breton, his relative, "a little more than kin and less than kind," who had also become possessed of other Hereward estates. Oger does not appear to have ventured any attack upon Hereward, and probably kept out of his way ; for Hereward not only held his own in Lincolnshire, but gave no peace to Warrenne and Taillebois, and harried the Normans in all the counties of Mercia, where lands formerly belonging to Alfgar, Edwin, and Morcar were situated. He had no lack of Saxon supporters, for was he not the representative of the Saxon cause in England ? But he relied chiefly upon the justness of his cause, and upon his own energy and ability.

The extent of woodland at this time in England was probably one third of the total area. The woods supplied timber, largely used in house building, fuel and furniture, besides arms and implements of husbandry. Excellent pasture, also acorns, beech mast, and berries fit for food were obtained in profusion. Herds of cattle and pigs were kept in these woods for the best part of the year, and in connection with this service lodges, or sheds, were constructed by the herdsmen in their leisure.

[1] They may have taken advantage of Hereward's temporary absence from the camp. He was too straightforward to suspect his allies of treachery.

Except in summer, these primeval forests were gloomy and unfrequented :

> "The woodland wide, with bushes thick around,
> And gloomy ilex hid the adjacent ground;
> An undergrowth of brambles barred the way
> Through paths obscure in the dim light of day."[1]

To a skilled strategist like Hereward the means of evading and retaliating upon an unwary foe in the ambush afforded by the cover of the Morkery woods was quite as good a position as the fens of Ely. The lodges, shifted from week to week, afforded excellent shelter, and to those who so well knew the country, and were as skilful with the bow as in training hawk and hound, food was easily procurable. This was the beginning of that forest life destined to be the resort of the persecuted, the friendless, and the outlaw, until Sherwood Forest rang with the name of Robin, the outlawed Earl of Huntingdon, and his frères. When men were hard as nails, and fighting the condition of existence, who shall say that life under the greenwood tree, though sometimes a short and a merry one, did not possess the highest charms? At any rate, Hereward was the first king of the forest glade who sang,

> "I roam at will o'er mead or hill,
> Or deep and deep in the woodland shade,
> With my good yew bow
> In my hand I go,
> As free as the bird or the wild red roe,"[2]

when not engaged in harrying the enemy, and organizing a successful, though guerilla warfare. The war was carried into the counties of Cambridge, Huntingdon, Northampton, Leicester and Warwick, and no force could be raised able to cope with Hereward's strength and strategy. At length he was able to capture Ivo de Taillebois,[3] upon whom William had

---

[1] "Silva fuit late dumis atque ilice nigra
Horrida, quam densi complerant undique sentes :
Rara per occultos ducebat semita calles."—*Æneid*, ix., 381.

[2] Until the seventeenth century the red deer were found in all forests and parks. They were always wild and intractable, and are now generally replaced in England by the more docile fallow deer and the spotted zebra variety. In some parks (Donnington Hall) there are six or seven varieties of deer.

[3] Ivo de Taillebois, Tailgebosc, or Taylbois, called himself Count of Anjou! He was a favourite of William's, a wood-tax gatherer by trade, but

The Camp of Refuge. 41

conferred large estates, and an opportunity was afforded Hereward to make peace with William, as he had now other plans in view, and further resistance was absolutely futile, as William's authority prevailed from the Grampians to the southern coast. Accordingly negotiations were entered upon, resulting in the restitution of Hereward's lands, and his acknowledgment of William's lawful authority, " according to the laws of Alfred and Edward."

Hereward's surrender upon the honourable terms accorded him by William was in strict accordance with the laws of honour, and in the best interests of the Saxons, whose cause he espoused. The latter were numerous, but badly armed and much weakened by exposure and privation, whilst the strength of the Norman men-at-arms increased daily. As a recognised land-holder, Hereward would still have the power to save his people from famine and extermination. He was not in such a strait as the hero who cried : "All is lost except honour." A *pied à terre* was restored to him, whereas from a military point of view he had no *point d'appui* upon which to rally his forces. Subsequent history shows that he did not care to retain the lands as an under-tenant except Pebwith (Bedworth), at Marston Jabet, of which he may have obtained the fee. Under the circumstances the course he adopted was strictly in accordance with military usage then or now, and not less patriotic than his previous resistance.

Hereward, who seems to have found time for everything, had fallen in love a second time with a Saxon lady of large estates and wealth, named Ælfthryth. His first wife Torfrida was probably dead, as Freeman suggests in his " History of the Norman Conquest." Nothing more is heard of her after she entered the convent, nor is there any mention of her taking holy vows. Hereward seems to have been free to marry again, and according to the rhymer, the lady was yet more eager. The brilliancy of Hereward's exploits had no doubt reached Ælfthryth in Worcestershire, where she appears to have been a ward or tenant of good Bishop Wulfstan.

---

obtained all the forfeited estates of Edwin and Morcar in Lincolnshire, with their sister Lucy, who was forced to become his wife. See Appendix : " Lucia."

Whilst he was yet engaged in a fierce struggle with the Normans, the lady could not resist sending him a cartel of congratulations, and intimating her sense of his manly and virtuous superiority.

The chronicler[1] thus tells the tale : " It is not clear why Hereward delayed accepting Ælfthryth's invitation; the natural inference is that his negotiations then pending with William were of primary importance."

> "Par plusieurs anz tant guerroia
> Si qe une dame le manda,
> Que de li ont oi parler;
> Par meinte foiz l'ad fet mander
> Que lui vensist, si le plesoit;
> L'onor son prière il dorroit;
> Et, s'il la pernoit à muiller,
> Bien porroit François guerreier.
> Ceo fut Alftrued (Ælfthryth) qe ço manda
> A Ereward, qe mult ama :
> Par plusieurs foix tant le manda
> Qe Ereward s'apresta."

Free Translation.

> "Thus year by year he fought so well,
> The rhymers all his praises tell,
> Until fair Ælfthryth's yielding heart
> Was struck by Cupid's burning dart ;
> And so at last she prayed him come,
> If it so pleased him, to her home ;
> For Hereward she loved full well,
> And would her true love to him tell ;
> Yet often though she told her love,
> It seemed no power his heart could move ;
> At length her prayers were heard above,
> And Hereward hastened to his love."

In 1086 Hereward held a knight's fee in land at Evenlode,[2] in Worcestershire, under the Bishop. This may have been a

---

[1] Geoff. Gaimar, "Chron. Ang. Norm.," i., 22.

[2] Evenlod, or Evenlode, was in Henry II.'s time the site of the little nunnery called Godeston, to which Fair Rosamond, mistress of Henry II., retired and died. She was a daughter of the Baron de Clifford. Her history, founded on fact, is woven in romance. The clue of silk and the poison-bowl of the jealous Queen Eleanor are modern additions. The chronicler Brompton, *temp.* Edward II., one hundred and fifty years after the event, first wrote of the "puella spectatissima" for whom the secret bower near "Wodestocke" was devised "ne forsan a regina facile deprehenderetur."

portion of Ælfthryth's estate, or may have been given by Wulfstan,[1] a worthy Saxon prelate.

There is every reason to believe that Hereward's marriage with Ælfthryth was a happy one, and more suitable to both of them than Hereward's previous marriage to a foreign lady, though both his wives appear to have possessed admirable charms and the highest qualifications. Hereward's chief family appears to have sprung from his second marriage, and this must have been a further source of mutual happiness. Had we been able to obtain Hereward's personal opinion he might have said :

> "Beshrew me, for I love her heartily ;
> For she is wise, if I can judge her,
> And fair she is, if that mine eyes be true,
> And true she is, as she has proved herself,
> And therefore, like herself, wise, fair, and true,
> Shall she be placed in my constant soul."

Hereward, though now past his early manhood, was well entitled to enjoy the love and happiness which accords with the Spanish sentiment at the head of the next chapter, and is especially the reward of the brave.

At length, therefore, he obtained well-earned rest, a truce from incessant warfare, a loving wife of his own nation, and the restoration of a considerable part of his own estates. William de Warrenne and Ivo de Taillebois, with other Norman adventurers, still looked upon him as a "malignant," as the coarse republicans of a later date looked upon the gentlemen of England. But here for the present we will leave Hereward, settled again on the estates of his fathers, and founding a home and a name for his descendants.

[1] Wulfstan had been installed Bishop against his wish by Edward the Confessor. He was no doubt a personal friend of Leofric ; he fought against William at Senlac, but afterwards swore allegiance to him, when he perceived that resistance was unavailing, and only tended to prolong civil dissensions. He would in his heart have desired to aid Hereward, and Wulfstan may not only have aided his reconciliation to the King, but have provided him with a wife and an estate. The Bishop was born at Long Itchington, in Warwickshire, and must have been acquainted with Hereward's family.

Chapter v.

Hereward: the War in Maine; Domestic Life; his End.

> "His square-turned joints and strength of limb
> Showed him no carpet knight so trim,
> But in close fight a champion grim,
> In camps a leader sage."
>   SCOTT's *Marmion.*

> "Porque hum velho idoso,
> Feio e muito socegado,
> Se na guerra tem boa fama,
> Com a mais fermosa dama
> Merece de ser ditoso."
>   *Spanish Ballad.*

(*Translation:* "A man who has earned a goodly fame in war, let him be ever so old, ugly, and broken down, is worthy to be happy with the most beautiful of women, proving courage to be the most estimable of qualities, and most admired by the ladies.")

IVES of adventure are seldom extended; but there is every reason to believe that Hereward was spared to pass through another campaign after his patriotic struggle for the freedom of England from a foreign yoke in the island of Ely, and that he ended his days peacefully, after a stormy life, transmitting his name, his virtues, and his estates to his descendants through his second marriage with the Saxon lady Ælfthryth.

Sometimes Hereward, attended by his old comrade Ibe Winter (who settled in Norfolk, and whose descendants called their Bultees estate "Herewards," and left it to that family), another friend or two, and their serving-men, passed between Evenlode and Hereward's castle at Coleshill, county Warwick, to visit his mother at Kingsbury Hall, the old residence of a line of Mercian kings, occupied some time by Ethelfleda, King Alfred's daughter, whilst she superintended the raising of the strong and regal tower of Tamworth. On the cliff above the Tame, where the site shows what an important post of defence Kingsbury held, may still be seen the remains of the moat; and its associations with a long line of Saxon Kings renders it dear to antiquaries.

It is not improbable that Hereward found it difficult to hold his Warwickshire lands under the Earl of Mellent. A hundred years later we find the old Warwickshire estates abandoned, and one branch of the family settled at Pebworth,[1] near Marston Jabet, and at Terrington in Norfolk, under Roger Bigod,[2] Earl of Norfolk. Hereward, always a soldier first, must have found more congenial occupation in the expedition to Maine (Gaimar, "Chron. Ang. Norm.," i., 22, 23) in 1074, when he was invited, or ordered, to accompany William in command of the English troops.[3] Referring to this subject, Freeman, the historian of the Norman Conquest, says: "The host which he led consisted largely of his English subjects. . . . stranger than all is the thought, probable, at least, if not certain, that the captain of the English band was no other than the most stout-hearted of living Englishmen, even Hereward himself."

Few details are left us of the prowess of the English arms in Normandy, but we know they contributed largely to the restoration of William's revolted towns. Subsequent to the fall of Ely, the chronicles appear less accurate in regard to

[1] See pedigree, chapter x., p. 9, Heralds' Visitation, 1619, Harleian Pub., vol. xii.

[2] "L'Ancestre Hue le Bigot
Ki avoit terre a Maletot
Etais Loges et Chanon."—*Roman de la Rose*, i. 1377.
Appendix: Roger le Bigod.

[3] At this time the Saxon army was called "fyrd," but in the Chronicle of Florence Wigorn of this date the troops assembled were called "Here." It is a slight point, but Hereward's name may have caused the change of terms.

Hereward's history, and we can only be guided by probabilities in connection with the actual data of Domesday, in 1086, and the subsequent position of the family in the twelfth century.

After the expedition of Maine, Hereward's fighting days were over. True to his promise to the King, he never again took up arms against him. The castle at Coleshill was probably left a ruin in the hands of Mellent; and even that interesting wooden structure[1] in the fens of Ely, where at the beginning of the troubles he had received Edwin, Morcar and Waltheof, and with them decided upon the plan of the campaign, had succumbed to decay and the ravages of time.

The chronicle of Geoffrey Gaimar gives a tragic ending to the life of the Saxon hero, which is repeated by the writer in "de Hydâ." It refers to names and facts in a circumstantial manner, but it would have been such a stain upon William's character, that it is impossible to credit the story. It is also opposed to the more probable account in the "Gesta," 89-98 : "Herewardus igitur, miles insignis et in multis locis expertus et cognitus, a Rege in gratiam susceptus, cum terris et possessionibus patris sui multis post modum vixit annis, Regi Willelmo fideliter serviens ac devote compatriotis placens et amicis ; ac sic demum quevit in pace, cujus anime propitietur Deus. Amen." All of which is confirmed by Domesday and subsequent records. The rhymer, however, thus describes in a remarkably graphic and circumstantial manner an attack upon Hereward, led by Ralph de Dol, with an overpowering number of assailants :

> "Od s'espée iiij en occist,
> Dès qu'il fiert le bois retentist ;
> Mès donc brusa le brant d'ascer
> Desus l'elme d'un chevalier
> Et il l'escu en ses mains prist
> Si en fiert qe ij Francais occist ;
> Mes iiij vindrent à son dos
> Qui l'ont feru par mi le cors,
> Od iiij lances l'ont féru ;
> N'est merveille s'il est cheu."—GEOFFREY GAIMAR, i., 26.

---

[1] "Castreum ligneum in ipsis paludibus construcerunt quod usque in hodiernum diem castellum Herewardi a comprovincialibus nuncupatur."— Roger of Wendover's (ii., 9) account of the castle bearing Hereward's name at the Camp of Refuge.

Translation.
"His sharp-edged sword four foes laid low,
He fiercely held the wood below;
But then, alas! that brand of steel
On a knight's helmet broke at heel.
In both his hands he took his shield,
And crushed two Frenchmen ere they yield,
Whilst four behind him stealing round
Press the brave hero to the ground;
Four spears well-pointed strike the blows—
What wonder that his life-blood flows."

Ralph de Dol was one of those crushed by the shield, and he and Hereward, overpowered by numbers, fell dead together. Then one Asselin strikes off Hereward's head, praising his valour and his prowess:

"Mès Alselin[1] le paroccist
Cil de Ereward le chef prist,
Se jura Dieu et sa vertu,
Et li autre qui l'ont véu
Par meinte foiz l'ont fort juré
Que onques si hardi ne fut trouvé;
Et s'il eust eu od lui trois,
Ma i entrassent li Francois;
Et si'l ne fut issis occis
Tous les chaçast fors del pais."—GEOFFREY GAIMAR.

Translation.
"But Asselin, the parricide,
Swore by heaven and all beside,
As if chief priest to Hereward,
To valour giving due regard;
Repeatedly declared and swore
So brave a man ne'er lived before;
And if but three such in the land,
They would have killed the whole French band;
Or if such men were only found,
They'd drive the French from English ground."—H.

Such is the legendary account of the dramatic and tragic fate of Hereward. It is, however, rather too much in the style of the chorus of a Greek play to bear the impress of truth and fact, and although the apotheosis of a hero, as in the "Morte d'Arthur," affords a grander climax, in Hereward's case the facts constrain us to look for a more commonplace ending of his remarkable career. At the same time this legend rests

[1] The only Ascelin known to be with William was Ascelin, surnamed Gouel de Perceval, alleged ancestor of the Earls of Egmont.

upon authority as good as other incidents we have accepted, and the reader is at liberty to draw his own conclusions. The massacre, if it took place, was probably in the days of the red-haired William II., who appears to have had less compunction and to have been rather more cruel and unscrupulous than his father. There is much probability and sufficient evidence to support the fact that the noble old chief sank to a peaceful grave, not without a sure and certain hope to be realized hereafter. He shed no innocent blood, but fought in defence of hearth and home, and to maintain the honour of his country. As a true knight, he served William faithfully after he acknowledged his authority, and never broke an oath or an engagement. He sought neither reward nor distinction, and would not condescend to preserve his own possessions at the expense of his country.

As a soldier, William did not fail to appreciate the character of this renowned Saxon, and it will live to his credit in history that Hereward was treated honourably and his lands restored.

His lineal descendants, of whom we find due records,[1] were probably descended from his second wife, whilst his daughter Torfrida, who married a Norman, Hugh de Evermue, was the offspring of the first marriage, bearing her mother's name. Of the descendants who settled in Warwickshire and Norfolk we shall speak hereafter. A deliberate attempt appears to have been made by heralds and historians to conceal the fact and existence of Hereward's descendants, and it was not until the record of the "Great Book of Ely" was referred to, that indubitable evidence of such legitimate descendants was proved. As a matter of fact, there were more Herewards during the Plantagenet period than there are now Harwards. It would indeed have been a matter of regret if no descendant had remained to record the principal events of his life, his gallant conduct and undoubted patriotism, which must ever remain inseparable from English history.

The pious bequest of Hereward's grandson, who, with his wife Wilburga, devised a carucate[2] of land at Terrington

[1] In the "History of Norfolk" (Blomefield's), the "Liber Ecclesiæ Eliensis," and the Herald's Visitation.

[2] The same as a plough, or a hide of land, about one hundred and sixty acres, one-fifth of a knight's fee. As much land as may be eyred and tilled in a year and a day with one plough.

His End. 49

(Taunton), Norfolk, to the church of Len (Lynn) for prayers to be said for the souls of Hereward his father, and of Hereward the banished, or the exile, his grandfather, affords an important link in the family, and clear proof that he left a family and heirs male.

We find four hundred years later that, owing to a failure of heirs male, the Norfolk estates passed into the hands of a Suffolk family named Hamond-Claxton,[1] of Great Livermore, whilst the lineal Warwickshire branch, finding the rich alluvial lands of the Severn valley preferable to the lighter lands on the Avon, emigrated to Hartlebury, where they were the chief residents in the time of good Queen Bess,[2] and have been well known in the counties of Worcestershire and Gloucestershire to the present day.

Branches of this family settled at Harvington[3] and Bretforton, but their estates, devolving upon heiresses, passed by marriage into other families. Sketch pedigrees of these branches will be found in the Appendix of Pedigrees.

[1] The personal name Clac is found in Domesday Book; it is derived from Old Norse *klaka*, from *klaka*, to twitter like a swallow. In Danish the estate of this family was Claxby, in Saxon Claxton, from which the more recent name is derived.

[2] See the deed of enfeofment of Hartlebury Grammar School by Queen Elizabeth.

[3] See Nash's "History of Worcestershire" and Grazebrook's "Heraldry of Worcestershire."

Chapter vj.

Etymology and Orthography of Hereward.

"Far dearer the grave or the prison
Illumined by one patriot name,
Than the trophies of all who have risen
On Liberty's ruins to fame."
                                MOORE.

"He will keep that good name still."
                    Henry V., Act iii., Sc. 7.

N fitting together the connecting links of an ancient family history, we may be sure to find that the spelling of names has varied in the course of centuries with the changes which have occurred in the language of the country, and it would be strange indeed if names of Teutonic or Scandinavian origin did not experience some change in form while passing from the Gothic through the Old Saxon or Danish, afterwards corrupted with Anglo-Norman and Middle English, up to our own time.[1]

In studying these changes it is not only necessary to support the presumption of legitimate orthographical modifications by tangible and contemporary proof, but also to observe that no change is occasioned thereby in the meaning or etymology of the name under consideration. In this contention, the evidence now adduced, in addition to the known rules of spelling and pronunciation, will be found in the

---

[1] Professor Max Müller traces the periods when some of the Hindoo Shastras were written by the construction of the Sanscrit text—a rare feat of philology when the almost mythical period is considered.

Etymology and Orthography of Hereward. 51

inscriptions upon coeval coins, the use or disuse of the letter *w* in the earlier period of English history, especially in words of Scandinavian origin, and in the method of writing shown to be in use during that period.

Under certain circumstances a name may become so changed as to be unrecognisable; but such a change can only take place legitimately when the language of the country has completely changed; thus, the name of the barbarian Visigoth Theodoric, in the Gothic period, becomes Dietricht in the High German of the modern historian.[1]

The peerage and family histories in England contain many instances where a complete change of name is alleged to have occurred inconsistent with the laws of orthography and etymology. In such cases the presumption arises of a desire to merge a somewhat vulgar name in a more aristocratic patronymic; and we may find that more than one distinguished family has endeavoured to connect itself with the noble lineage of Hereward by a similar process.

In the Saxon name "Hereward," now spelt according to the Danish form "Harward," some slight variations in spelling have occurred. The most ancient and Scandinavian form is "Harvard," becoming in Teutonic shape "Herevald," "Herevard," "Hervard." More recently the *v* became *w;* but the Bishops of Sherburne, A.D. 750, and of Llandaff, A.D. 1056, both spelt the name "Herewald." So late as the ninth century the Archbishops of Canterbury, Vulfred, 830, Vigmund, 854, and Vielfhen, 895, preferred the *v* to the *w*, and the name William was sometimes spelt Lvillem in the twelfth century.[2]

The changes in spelling "Hereward" which have occurred are simple and can be clearly explained, being quite consistent with the laws of etymology; a greater difficulty lies in the disproof of alleged rights preferred by claimants more or less illustrious to a common ancestry with Hereward, the brave Saxon, and his family. As it is impossible to prove a negative,

[1] This is fully explained by Sir Monier Williams in his preface to vol. x. of Kingsley's works, "The Roman and the Teuton." He gives eighty-six varieties of spelling the name "Theodoric," all consistent with its etymology.

[2] See silver pennies and stycæ of the Archbishops, and penny of William, second son of King Stephen.

52 *Herewardi Arbor Gentis.*

it will rest with our readers to decide, when we come to discuss the Doubtful Claimants of the Lineage, whether the evidence recorded is untainted and founded on fact, or whether it breaks down under analysis and the weight of evidence against it.

When the Hereward family emigrated with other Saxon colonists, " Here " and " Her " had the same signification in Germany, meaning an army; but in the Scandinavian tongue the same word was spelt " Har."[1] In England the more ancient form of spelling " Harvard " was in frequent use, especially during the Danish invasion, and " Harward " was the correctly modified form of " Hereward " or " Herward " in the fifteenth century. The Norfolk branch wrote the name " de Hereward," " Hereward," and latterly " Herward "[2] and " Harward." The offshoot in Southwark adopted the Danish spelling " Harvard." In Warwickshire the name was always spelt " Hereward," and in Worcestershire until the fifteenth century, when it was changed to " Harward."[3]

During the period of Danish ascendency, between 787 and 1040, the name appears to have been generally spelt " Harvard," sometimes erroneously written " Haward "; the letter *r* being then one stroke, written thus ɼ, and it might appear before *v* as the first stroke of a *w* (𝔴) in Old English character. That letter was, however, almost unknown and certainly unused in the old Danish language.[4] At the time of Edward the Confessor the name was spelt " Hereward " in accordance with the Continental fashion in Germany of that period.

The generally accepted derivation of the names " Hereward," " Herward," or " Harward," is " here," " her," or " har " (Danish), an army, and " ward " or " vard," a guard. " Har "

[1] See the " Canterbury Chronicle." The Danes were styled " Northmen from Herethaland," which is Hardeland, in Jutland, in Danish orthography. The *th* becomes *d* in Danish.

[2] The inscription on a brass tablet in the church of Boton, Norfolk, is: " Orate pro anm̄a Johanni Herward qui obiit XVI. die Aprilis cujus anm̄a propicietur Deus. Amen." See Blomefield's " History of the County of Norfolk."

[3] See brass in church of St. Cross, Winchester, in chancel, date 1493.

[4] The modern names Westwick, Windham, Wareham, Wellingham, were Vestervik, Vindeholm, Vare, Velling.

Etymology and Orthography of Hereward. 53

is, however, literally a warrior in the north, "hari" or "here" in Germany, and the plural of warrior is an army. A very old term for a sword was "hjørn," or "hirn," used in the north; "hairn," "hern" in the Gothic; "heorn" in Anglo-Saxon; hence "Heornvard," or "Hereward," spelt "Hereuuard," the sword-guardian. The oldest mention of the name was by Tacitus, as Chariovalda, a Batavian prince. Hence we derive "Harivald," warrior-power, abbreviated to "Heriold" and "Harald" in the north. It was always a most renowned northern name.[1] It is certainly a surname referring to military attributes, derived probably from one of the heathen gods, Ares, son of Zeus, and Here, god of war (Mars), through the Greek,[3] as Ariovistus, or from a Scandinavian name "Har," for Wodin or Odin, the patron of the ancient Germans, and their tutelary god in war. For many centuries war was so essentially the pursuit and life occupation of the German race, that the name "Hereward," signifying a leader in war, could not have been inappropriate. It referred probably to an office as marshal or general; an ealderman was sometimes called "heretoga."

In the margin are noted the names known to us, which are clearly derived from the same roots and the same etymology. We have now to consider their orthography and whether the varieties of spelling can be duly accounted for. "Herewald" was the form of spelling used by both the Bishops of Sherburne, A.D. 736-773, and Llandaff, 1056, died 1104, of whom more hereafter.

1. HEREWALD.
2. HARVARD.
3. { HEREWARD. HERWARD. HARWARD. }
4. { HERWART. HERVART. }
5. { HELWALD. HERWALD. }

The Bishop of Sherburne was one of the earliest descendants of the Saxon colonists of this family, and died shortly before the Danish troubles began. Hereward, the great soldier and patriot, was by no means the first of his race in England. The Bishop was equal in rank with the Earl, and next to the King, to whom he was both adviser and a friend, was necessarily a man of learning and culture, and no doubt his name was spelt correctly. Why, then, did he use an *l* in place of the second *r*? Such interchange was not un-

---
[1] These derivations are taken chiefly from Miss Charlotte Yonge's "Christian Names."
[2] See Appendix: Greek derivation of "Here."

usual in the harsh Teutonic language. Referring to a coin of that period, we find Æthilheard, Archbishop of Canterbury 790 A.D., when Offa was King of Mercia. Ruding's "Annals of the Coinage of the United Kingdom," the best textbook on the subject, shows the Archbishop's name spelt on his coins both Edilvard and Edelvald, proving the *r* and *l* were interchangeable, as well as *e* and *i* in some cases.[1] It must be noted that the Danish invasion occurred in Æthilheard's time, and the coins referred to were probably struck during the latter part of his life, which accounts for the Danish spelling. "Æthilheard" is pure Saxon, "Edilvard" and "Edelvald" the same name in Danish guise. Observe, also, the substitution of *d* for *th* in this case, as in note 1, p. 52, "Hardeland" for "Herethaland."

It is probable that the Archbishop's name was also spelt Æthilward and Æthilvard, and that *w* for *v* may have been substituted in Hereward's name at a later period.

The second name on the list is "Harvard,"[2] sometimes erroneously written "Haward." The cause of this error has already been explained.[3] It is clearly Danish spelling and appears to have been in vogue after the Danish invasion until the tenth century, and was probably adopted from motives of expediency or fashion. The Herewards and Harvards appear to have held as high a position under the Danish government as under the Saxons. "Eadgith" or "Ediva," sometimes written "Godgifu" or "Godiva,"[4] the mother of Hereward of Ely, is known to have been a relation of Duke Oslac, a cousin of the reigning house, who rose to such eminence in Edgar's reign. Oslac was descended from Oslac, the Danish cup-bearer of Ethelwulf, who married Oslac's

---

[1] Refer to coins of Offa (757-796 A.D.), Supplement to Ruding's "Annals of the Coinage of Great Britain and its Dependencies from the Earliest Period of Authentic History to the Reign of Victoria," chapter iv.; reverse Edilvard and Offa; Ruding, 5, 26, reverse Edelvald.

[2] This spelling was adopted about 1637 by Jno. Harvard, founder and benefactor of Harvard University, Boston, Massachusetts, sometime of Boar's Head Court, of St. Mary Overies, London.

[3] See p. 52.

[4] The *g* is not sounded, so these names are pronounced "Edith," "Ediva,' "Odifa," or "Odiva," and are meant for the same name.

Etymology and Orthography of Hereward. 55

daughter Osburga, whose four sons and seven of their lineal descendants, all Kings of England, were of kin to Duke Oslac and Hereward's mother.[1] The position of Oslac was no doubt materially strengthened during the Danish invasion, and Hereward's ancestry must have been nobles of the highest rank. In the tenth century, during Danish rule, the rank of the Harvard of that period was second only to the Danish under-kings.[2]

"Haward" is neither Saxon nor Danish, but a corrupt spelling of "Harvard." It cannot be a misspelling for Hayward, as that officer was only called into existence at the Norman Conquest nominally as a rural bailiff (*haie*, Fr., a hedge), but really to squeeze the Saxon cultivators. "Harvard" was a common name[3] amongst the Northmen. Taken by the settlers with Rollo in Neustria, it became "Houard" in Normandy, and "Howard," or "Howardus," in England (see Domesday). All these names are synonymous with "Huard," or "Hugichard," signifying firm in mind or thought, from Scan. *hargr*, same as "hir" still used. "Ha" or "haa" was pronounced "ho." "Haghen," "Hagano," or "Hogni" is the villain of the Nibelungen.

"Hereward" and "Herward" are both spelt correctly in Saxon form, Anglicized so far as the *w* is concerned. Both in Denmark and Germany the names would have been written "Herevard" and "Hervard." "Harward" takes the Danish "Har" for "Here," and is probably the more ancient form of the name.

[1] This lady was sister of Thorold (a distinct Danish name), Sheriff of Lincolnshire, and founder of Spalding Abbey. Of the same family was Thorold, Sheriff in the time of Coenwlf (Kenulph), 794-818, King of Mercia.

[2] In the witangemote, or council, at Lewton, 931 A.D., Orm and Guthrum, both under-kings, signed before Harvard, who was third Dux. At Colchester, same year, Harvard signs next to Guthrum and Thurum in a council of 94 notables—viz., 2 archbishops, 2 under-kings, 17 bishops, 15 duces, and 58 ministers, or comes.

[3] A family of some note of this name settled in county Brecknock, North Wales, at Heolvanog, "the lofty brow," since at Court Sion Young (John Young's Court). They were also seated at Frwdgrech, which went to the Lewises and Williamses by marriage; also at Newton, which passed by marriage to Sir J. Games. Pont Wilyn, now a farmhouse, was once their estate.

"Herwart," or "Hervart,"[1] is the same name spelt in Bavaria in the sixteenth and seventeenth centuries. John Frederick Herwart was Chancellor of Bavaria in the early part of the seventeenth century, and the author of some well-known works.[2]

The last legitimate cognomen is Von Helwald, or Herwald. This is the modern name as now borne by the German branch of the family, of which there are several distinguished members in Berlin and the provinces. Major Von Helwald is the author of a valuable work on Central Asia.

Besides the names given in this list, there are none that will bear etymological analysis, or can be traced to a common origin with Hereward or Harward. In a subsequent chapter the claims of all other aspirants to consanguinity will be duly considered. None of them can be fairly established. One gentleman declares his family inherited the nickname of Hereward, much as if families named Bald, Fat, or Simple, claimed royal descent from the Carlovingian Kings of France through those distinguishing additions to the name of Charles.

Hereward's alleged nickname "the Wake" will be briefly noticed hereafter, but there is not the slightest proof that he ever had a nickname, such being an after-thought of John, a monk of Peterborough in the fifteenth century. Hereward did not require another name to distinguish him in his generation. From his known character a nickname would have been resented if repeated in his hearing. His own name without addition or prefix[3] stands out as the most illustrious of his time and country, and a bright example to his fellow-countrymen in future ages.

[1] "Wart," "warten," in Germany, is "vordhr" in the north; in French, "garde," "gardien." "Wart" in Germany is "ward" in England, and "vard" in the north. A defender was Saxon "weard," guard, warden.

[2] "Chronologia Nova et Vera," 2 parts, 4to., 1622-26, and "Admiranda Ethica Theologica Mysteria," and others.

[3] The Herewards of Norfolk and Warwickshire sometimes used the prefix "de," but rarely; they did not acquire their name from their settlement, but gave it to their lands; and besides estates in Surrey, Sussex (near East Grinstead), and Warwickshire, one of their estates in Norfolk (see Blomefield) was called Herewards. The Norman prefix "de" was used in a ridiculous manner; thus Ivo de Taillebois was lord of the wood-tax, a very common toll-collector.

Chapter vij.

Doubtful Claimants of the Lineage.

"Nam genus et proavos et quæ non fecimus ipsi,
Vix ea nostra voco."
OVID.

"Respectable ancestors, hard things to buy,
To order are made, or filched on the sly."
See Heralds' Visitations, 1551-85.

NCESTORS, however illustrious, are in no sense individual property. Their noble qualities are left to us to maintain and exemplify in our own time, and to distribute as widely as possible. Far is it from our intention to confine or monopolize the Hereward pedigree, but history, whether family or national, requires a thorough sifting of alleged facts, especially when they rest on insecure and inaccurate foundations.

It is not our desire to attempt to decide upon the many claims which have been made to consanguinity with the Hereward family. Such claims should rest upon their own merits. We wish to discuss those claims as impartially as others which we have proved to be well-established, and we shall be prepared to give the same prominence to any statement in support of them. We now give a list of such claimants who have come under our notice, with *primâ facie*

evidence why we consider their claims to be badly founded and inadmissible.

Whilst some of the claimants endeavour to connect themselves with Hereward, others, still more lost in the clouds of historic doubt, hold themselves allied to Leofric, whom they call Earl of Chester or Leicester, no doubt referring to the great Earl of Mercia in the time of Edward the Confessor, the father of Alfgar of East Anglia, and of Hereward the renowned.[1]

1. { HAREWARD. HAREWOOD.
2. HARWOOD.
3. HAYWOOD.
4. { HORWODE. WHORWODE. WHORWOOD.
5. { HAYWARD. HAWARD.
6. HOWARD.
7. TEMPLE.
8. WAKE.

The names here given in the margin are nearly all subsequent to the Norman Conquest, and we hold that they are not only doubtful claimants of the lineage of Hereward, but that it is impossible to prove they even belonged to the same family. Some of these names represent branches in various parts of England, but we shall here consider the name only. Most of these names, except the two last, can be divided into two classes, and it will be seen that they are derived from offices held under the Norman Forest Laws or agricultural system; the names ending in "wode" or "wood" coming under the first category, and those ending in "ward" being offices of husbandry.

In the first case we shall find confirmation of this statement in the registered armorial bearings of Harwood of Hagbourne and Streatley, one of the most ancient and respectable of these families. Their arms are: Argent, a chevron between three stags' heads, caboshed gules. These are clearly the bearings of an officer possessing power and privilege under the Forest Laws.[2]

Still further indication is afforded of the right meaning of the name by the crest of the same family, which is: On a wreath, a stag's head caboshed, gules, having in its mouth an oak bough proper, acorned, or. Here is literally the "wood" typified by the oak bough and acorn, in addition to the forest-warder's emblem of the stag's head.

[1] See Sir Henry Ellis, ii., 146, and "Chron. Ang.-Norm.," ii., xi. England was divided into three great earldoms in Edward the Confessor's time—Northumbria, Mercia, and Wessex.

[2] Stanley, Earl of Derby, bears three stags' heads for the bailiwick of Wirrall, or Wyrall, Forest.

The same name "Harwood" was spelt "Horwode," or "Whorwode," and "Whorwood," up to the end of the fourteenth century. The forest officers were nearly all of Norman extraction. They were of several grades—wardens, verdurers, foresters, etc. Those of the highest rank had great power, and the privilege of killing game, as well as of maiming dogs or cattle found in the preserve. Red-handed poachers suffered death.

Harewood is a mere descriptive name, met with in the northern counties, and best known as that of the estate of the De Lascelles family near Wetherby, in Yorkshire, from which they take the title of both the barony (1796) and earldom (1812).[1] The name "Harewood" dates back to the fifteenth century. There is no "Hareward," as the hare has never been afflicted with a separate legal existence apart from other ground game; but "Hayward" or "Haward," the latter being an abbreviation, is an ancient name, dating back nearly to the Norman Conquest, and indicating an officer appointed in each town, under the Norman laws, ostensibly to check the waste or injury of hedges,[2] in which the under-tenants had certain rights under the Saxon common law of hedge-bote, wood-bote, wood-geld. The appointment of this officer was a further exaction upon the Saxon peasants, who had to pay either bribes for permission to cut helves or staves, or fines for trespass.

It will be observed that none of the names above mentioned can be traced to a period before the Conquest, but they represent relics of the oppressive and vexatious Norman laws which for so many years curtailed the liberties of the English people.

"Howard,"[3] the Anglicised "Huard" or "Houard" of Neustria, is a name which may possibly have been known before the Conquest. Indeed, it seems not improbable that

[1] The arms of this family, sable a cross patonce, within a bordure or, the same as the device upon the seal of Sir Jno. Hereward, of Hedenham, county Norfolk, 1349; the cross patonce, or "patent," as Froissart calls it, is presumably that of Edward the Confessor.

[2] French, "haie," or "haye," a hedge; "La haye Sainte," the farm at Waterloo.

[3] Appendix: "Derivations of Howard."

the name of the antecessor of the noble houses of Norfolk, Carlisle, and Effingham is recorded in Domesday Book. Mr. Walter Rye, in a recent History of Norfolk, tells us that Chief Justice Sir W. Howard, who, according to Dugdale, was the first of his name, always spelt it "Haward."[1] According to Blomefield, the name "Howard" was first assumed by John, son of Sir William de Wigenhale, who was the Chief Justice. This was in the time of Henry III. In a list of wives of Henry VIII., written by Thomas Salwey, in a side-note to a copy of Hall's "Chronicles," 1550, in the library of Sir F. Winnington, of Stanford Court, he names "Cateryne Hauwarde."[2] Strange to say, the name "Howardus" recorded in Domesday is not referred to in the pedigree of the Duke of Norfolk, although "he was an honorable man,"[3] and of all those lines of descent claimed by this grasping family, there is none more probable than that through Howardus, who, with one Ulsus, both *liberi homines*, freemen, held land, presumably as under-tenants, at Navestock, in Essex. Freemen were usually ceorls and baseborn, but, if holding five ploughs, socas or carues of land, about eight hundred acres, they obtained the rank of thegn.

There is one reason strongly in favour of the presumption that the name, whether "le Howard," or "Haward," or "Hayward," was of Norman origin. The difference between the Saxon and the Latin races is still sufficiently marked not to be easily mistaken. The numerous portraits of the Howard family show no indication of Saxon origin, the men being dark in complexion, with a profusion of dark hair; the

[1] Two *Coram rege* rolls referred to by the heralds as mentioning William "de" Howard and William "Hauward" have each been tampered with to make them so read; the *le*, which was undoubtedly in the first, having been cut out, and the tail of the *y* in the second having been also removed with a knife to make "Hayward" read "Hauward." The pedigree contains numerous other fictions which have now been abandoned, except the claim to descent from Hereward, which we are now dealing with as utterly unfounded and inadmissible.

[2] Pennant, in his "Tour in Wales," suggests that the name is derived from Havarden or Hawarden Castle in Flintshire. The Havards in Wales were an ancient family. "Hawarden" was, however, "Hedoine," according to Domesday. See Appendix: "Hawarden Castle."

[3] He was a franklin, or freeman, if not a thegn.

Doubtful Claimants of the Lineage.

Saxon characteristic being a smooth cheek with very small beard.

The Howards have already paid dearly for their aspirations. That accomplished nobleman Henry Howard, K.G., Earl of Surrey, had the temerity to quarter the arms of Edward the Confessor,[1] for which offence of *lèse-majesté* he was promptly beheaded by Henry VIII., 1547.

As hereditary Earls Marshal of England successive Dukes of Norfolk have had exceptional opportunities of verifying their pedigree; and enriched with great wealth and high rank by the Crown, especially by that King they now call "iniquitous and tyrannical," they should have been most careful to avoid assuming honours to which they had a doubtful right, or tampering with their own pedigree or with those of others.

No weaker claim, or one supported by more unreliable evidence than that to the kinship of Hereward by the Duke of Norfolk as stated in the last editions of Burke's "Peerage," has ever been advanced. In earlier days Dugdale refused to support this claim, although employed, as he states,[2] to "manifest the greatness" of the Howards. He had not, however, the full courage of his opinions, for while avoiding any reference to the absolutely false statement that "Howard" and "Hereward" are one and the same name, he attributed his failure to trace a pedigree to Hereward solely to an alleged default of heirs male! Dugdale, after most careful research—for his character for accuracy is unimpeachable—was satisfied that the Chief Justice Sir W. Howard, 1308,[3] was the best ancestor the Howards could possibly produce. It is idle to suppose that Dugdale, the best antiquary and most accurate historian of his day, and whose chief sources of information were in Church records, should not have been well acquainted with the "Historia Ecclesiæ Eliensis," the book of the Church of Ely. He knew well that Hereward

[1] Evidently through his alleged kinship to the Hereward line. See Appendix: "Henry Howard, Earl of Surrey."
[2] See Burke's "Peerage," 1862, and Appendix: "Howard Claim."
[3] Sir William's father was John Howard, of Wiggenhall; married Lucy Germond. Perhaps the name is German, which would account at once for the *Saxon* pedigree.

and Howard were distinct names and families, and it would have been an insult to his truthful and accurate character to have pretended that one of these names could be put for the other.

However, Dugdale was thrown over and a new false claim advanced, in which the names Hereward and Howard were juggled about like the pea amongst the thimbles at a fair.[1] The grant of land in Torrington was made by a Hereward. That name has been spelt in England "Herward," "Harward" and "Hereward," but never "Howard." The arms borne by all true descendants of Hereward have nothing resembling the "cross crosslets" and "demi-lion rampant" of Howard.

If the Howards wish to extend the list of their legitimate ancestors, and claim Saxon descent, they can fall back upon the chief and only head of their name as recorded in Domesday, and add the escutcheon of Howardus of Navestock to other family achievements. The absurdity of their claims is proved by both the names appearing in Domesday, Hereward and Howardus, totally unconnected with each other.

The claim of the Temples through the late Duke of Buckingham, Lord Palmerston and Sir Grenville Temple is too weak and frivolous to be seriously entertained. Not even a *primâ facie* case is made out. The eagle of Leofric, Earl of Mercia is quartered on their arms, and the statement in support is to the effect that they obtained lands from the Knights Templars, from which they take the name of Temple, and *therefore they are entitled to bear the arms of Leofric.* Questionable logic surely. The Knights Templars had great powers. They could erect lists and conduct tournaments, trials by battle, and all feats of arms; they could grant asylum in their spiritual capacity, and as secular lords could free from debt or slavery. They may have acquired lands once held by Leofric; but even as his executors they had no power to confer his arms on strangers. Unless this claim is supported by much stronger proof than that advanced in the "Peerage" it ought to be withdrawn. As a matter of fact this family only came into notice and acquired property after the changes of the Reformation.[2]

[1] See Appendix: "Howard Claim," and Burke's "Peerage," 1867.
[2] See Nichols' "Herald and Genealogist," vol. iii., p. 385 : "Like other new-

Doubtful Claimants of the Lineage. 63

The last and weakest, not to say most ludicrous, claim we have to mention, is that of Wake, of Courteen Hall, Northampton. Charles Kingsley being terribly afflicted with the "cacoethes scribendi" of Catullus, wrote probably as much unintelligible nonsense as any author of his day. His utter incapacity as a professor of history was clearly exposed by various critics,[1] in the notices which appeared of his book called "Hereward the Wake : the last of the *English !*" The *Review* says "Mr. Kingsley's boast throughout is that he sticks close to the facts. For facts we venture to read fictions." As to the affix of "le Wake" to Hereward, on which nickname the Wakes found their claim to consanguinity, it was never heard of until the fifteenth century, when John of Peterborough used it for the first time. It is not mentioned in any of those records from which we derive our only historical facts regarding Hereward, neither by "Florence Wigorn," nor in the "De Gestis Herewardi," nor by the "Rhymers Gaimar," or Ingulph. The origin of "le Wake" or Wake-dog applies to a totally different person. When Fulk, Count of Anjou, was at war with Count Herbert of Maine (1015-36), the latter was so constant in his night attacks that even the dogs were kept awake by his frequent sallies, and Fulk's men-at-arms got no sleep. So Count Herbert was called the wake or wake-dog.[2] Good monk John of Peterborough little realized the temper of Hereward to suppose such a thing. Frederick de Warrenne[3] is said to have used contemptuous language to Hereward, refusing to acknowledge his knighthood, conferred by the Abbot of Peterborough, and not by a secular lord ; but William II. was knighted in the same manner by Lanfranc, Archbishop of Canterbury. The quarrel resulted in the wager of battle

---

made rich, when subjected to the patronage of flattering genealogists, the Temples have been furnished with an ancestry of the most remote and most ambitious kind that this country has to offer."

[1] See *Saturday Review*, May 19, 1866. Appendix: Kingsley's "Hereward the Wake."

[2] See Freeman's "Norman Conquest of England."

[3] Brother of William de Warrenne, said to have married Gundreda, stepdaughter of William I.

à *l'outrance* in which de Warrenne paid dearly for his temerity, and was slain.

It seems marvellous that good families, such as the Howards, Temples, and Wakes, who have benefited so largely by their Norman connection with "the powers that be," should envy the descendants of Hereward, oppressed and persecuted through generations of Norman and Plantagenet usurpers, for the heroic patriotism of their ancestor, until in the fourteenth and fifteenth centuries they found asylums in the Church, and in the peaceful avocations of country life ; Robert, 1330, as Archdeacon of Taunton and Prebend of Lincoln, William as Abbot of Circencester, and the Rev. Dr. Richard as Warden of St. Cross, 1430-93. Such futile claims to the name and reputation of a dead hero are an outrage upon chivalry. Less blame is due to individuals and families than to the heralds, whose especial duty it was to verify the claims brought before them. Except Dugdale and some of recent date these men appear to have been utterly unworthy of their position, and the so-called "Visitations," and the records in the Heralds' College derived from them, are in numerous cases untrustworthy and always suspicious. Then, as now, honours had to be paid for. The Battle Abbey Roll was being continually altered to find Norman ancestors for the Court favourites of the day, and the heralds appear, under the influence of largesse, to have been especially corrupt and venal.[1]

[1] The worst concoctions had their origin in the reign of Elizabeth, when Harvey, Glover, and other unscrupulous heralds forged and invented Norman ancestors for well-to-do families all over England : Harvey in thirteen counties (1551-67), and Glover in Yorkshire (1582-95).—"History of Norfolk," by W. Rye.

Chapter viij.

The Evidence of the Heralds.

"Arms and the man, I sing."
DRYDEN'S *Virgil.*

"The boast of heraldry, the pomp of power,
And all that beauty, all that wealth e'er gave;
Await alike the inevitable hour,
The path of glory leads but to the grave."
GRAY'S *Elegy.*

IT is a common experience to find heraldic works decry all illustrations in arms anterior to the Norman Conquest in England, and the reign of Hugues Capet in France, who is credited with the introduction of chivalry, an improved system of armour, and an extension of the mechanical arts. He is also said to have established the law of hereditary succession in titles and dignities, and therewith the family system of primogeniture.

Possibly he may have resuscitated some of these matters from the confusion resulting from the decadence of the Roman Empire. In that kingdom no privilege was esteemed more highly than that of hereditary right, and by Roman law at least one-fourth of the family property must be left to the children.[1] As to the use of armour and armorial ensigns, the

[1] See "Studies of Roman Law" by Lord Mackenzie, "Falcidian portion."

references to them in the Greek and Latin epic poems occur frequently.

In the Æneid, Book viii., line 588, we have :

"—— chlamyde et pictis conspectus in armis."
"Known by his mantling robe and blazoned arms."

And in Book vii., line 657 :

"—— clypeoque (gerit) insigne paternum."
"Paternal ensign on his shield he bore."

These instances might be multiplied indefinitely, and it is probable that from the earliest period a coloured ensign or device was borne before the chiefs in war.

In a previous chapter we have described the circumstances under which Hereward established a right to, and adopted the armorial coat of, Frederick de Warenne (Warren), brother to the Earl of Surrey, son-in-law of William, who was slain by him in fair combat according to the existing Saxon law of trial by battle.[1] By the laws of chivalry not only the life of the vanquished knight, but his arms and charger became the property of the victor; under the law of "trial by battle," the vanquished champion was treated as a recreant knight, and hung, whether he survived the combat or was slain.

The parti-coloured or chequy coat is a most ancient cognizance of undoubted Oriental origin, traceable to the parti-coloured coat worn by Joseph, the great-grandson of Abraham. It was adopted by Alfred the Great, in gold and gules, as the royal arms of England, impaled with Wales, Gules, three gryphons (or dragons) segreant or.[2] It will be found amongst the most ancient shields in France, and was probably used in Germany and the East at an earlier date.

Hereward's own device was the German eagle borne on a bend gules, the inherited arms of Leofric Earl of Mercia. The arms of Hereward and Harward of the counties of Warwick and Worcester as now borne and recorded in the Heralds' College are :

"1. Chequy or and azure, three eagles of the first displayed upon a bend gules. Crest, an eagle's head erased ppr."

[1] See Note 2, p. 34. [2] Harleian MSS., 4033.

The ascetic mind of Edward the Confessor discarded the brilliant coat of Alfred, and adopted the cross patonce or potent, between five martlets, a somewhat similar coat having been previously used by Ethelred II. It is evident that at that period, and until all armorial bearings were officially recorded in the twelfth century, devices were selected at the caprice of individuals, regardless of ancestral claims.

The late Duke of Buckingham in his coat of arms bore : " Second quarterly, first and fourth or, an eagle displayed sable for Leofric." His only claim to this cognizance appears to have been the marriage of his great-great-grandfather to Hester, afterwards Viscountess Cobham, ancestress of Lord Lyttleton of Hagley, and daughter of Sir R. Temple of Morlands, Hants. This family of Temple claim to have borne the eagle "since their ancestors were Earls of the Heptarch Kingdom of Mercia"; and they adduce a pedigree from Earl Edwin, the last Earl of Mercia, which is fiction, pure and simple, as Edwin was betrothed but never married, and died without legitimate issue.

Although the Duke of Buckingham cannot possibly have any other claim, except through the Temples, to the Hereward cognizance, yet he quarters for Temple second and third argent two bars sable, each charged with three martlets or, which have nothing to do with Leofric.

It has been already explained that this family only rose to notice after the Reformation. Should the Dukedom of Buckingham be revived, let us hope the Duke of the new creation will at least claim descent from someone born in wedlock.

At every step of a genealogical history the shortcomings of the Heralds' Office become more apparent. They knew well enough that Earl Edwin of Mercia died unmarried, and yet they record this mythical cognizance without even the bar sinister. We know that the periodical visitations of the heralds were undertaken more for the purpose of recording the arms and pedigrees of *nouveaux riches* and royal favourites than to secure the accurate registration of the most ancient and historic families. It is time these abuses should be discontinued, and that a public office should cease to disseminate barefaced fabrications.

During the early Norman dynasty the Herewards had enough to do to hold their own, and afford some protection to the English survivors of the Norman raid. Henry II. inaugurated a period of amnesty, and by his father's marriage with Matilda, grand-daughter of Margaret, sister of Edgar Atheling, an attempt was made to unite the Norman and Saxon races. Whether Matilda Plantagenet was the lawful representative of the royal house of England depends upon the fact whether Malcolm's first wife was dead when he married Margaret. History is not clear upon the point.[1] The alliance produced a season of calm, and the Herewards were treated with less jealousy and hostility. They ceased to be sub-tenants of Norman lords, and acquired several manors in Norfolk and lands in Warwickshire, near their old domains. It was not until the reign of Edward I. they were enabled to make a grant of land to the church of Len (Lynn, Norfolk) for the repose of the soul of the patriot, and in 1302 Robert Hereward served the office of Sheriff of the county of Norfolk. Edward III., in 1334, appointed another Robert, Archdeacon of Terrington, special commissioner to appear before the Pope at Avignon to claim the French crown, from which he was debarred by the Salique law. There is nothing to show that any Hereward desired Court favour or a place of profit. Their lives have always been characterised by simplicity and peace.

During the temporary successes of the House of York in the Wars of the Roses, Clement Hereward sat for Norwich, then the chief county constituency, in 1386 (9 Richard II.).[2] Clement was the great grandson of Robert, Sheriff in 33 Edward I.

In the fourteenth century we find several members of the family in holy orders. Sir John de Herwardstoke, of Sturston

[1] Malcolm's Danish wife was certainly dead, but there is not the same certainty about a Scotch lady who had a claim.

[2] Clement Hereward, M.P., of Aldburgh, by Will November 2, 1426, appoints John Bacon and Rich. Gegge trustees of his lands, Suffield, Wykmere, Wolferton, Matlass, Birmingham, Bulteas als. Herewards, West Hall, Penshippe, Guessmere, etc., for his wife and son Robert. Manor of Wykmere to wife for life, 100 marks to Margaret his daughter, £40 to Margery, daughter.

Hall Manor, was Rector of Pulham. He released the Sturston Hall Estate to his brother John, a citizen of London, in 1341, when instituted to the Rectory. Sir John sealed with "gules an eagle displayed or" on shield, his name round it. It will be seen hereafter the Norfolk family generally had adopted a different coat of arms.

John Hereward, possibly the same Sir John, was Rector of North Barsham in 1323. Another John Hereward was appointed Rector of Hedenham in 1340, and his son John succeeded him in the Rectory in 1372. A deed in the British Museum signed by the elder John Hereward is sealed with the cross patonce, the cognizance of Edward the Confessor. There is some doubt whether patonce, patent or potent, is the right description of this cross. Froissart says patent, Sir Bernard Burke potence, and a learned clerk of Oxford, well-versed in heraldic lore, gives potent as the correct orthography.

The elder branch of Herewards in Warwickshire continued to bear the ancient escutcheon, but the Norfolk branch adopted an entirely different coat of arms :

2. "Azure a fess gobonné gules and vert, between three owlets argent;" and this coat was borne by them with slight difference throughout the thirteenth to the fifteenth centuries.

William de Warenne's influence was paramount after the Bigots and Mowbrays, and this may have influenced many of the Herewards to change the device for the sake of peace. A difference in arms has often been made from mere caprice. The kings of France chose other bearings than the fleur-de-lys, which are only a modification of three toads displayed, adopted by Clovis. Francis had a salamander, other kings three crowns and three crescents, or a lion rampant, holding in his tail an eagle.[1]

It is impossible to account for these vagaries on the part of those entitled to bear hereditary achievements, except on the grounds of fancy or ignorance. These personal adoptions generally indicate the character of their owner. Louis XII. of France selected a hedgehog, with the words : "Qui s'y frotte s'y pique." "He who touches me pricks himself." Louis XIV., neglecting the lilies of France, created

[1] Refer to *Notes and Queries*, 1867, p. 122.

the device of "a sun darting its rays upon a globe," the motto, "Nec pluribus impar." Continual changes have been made in the royal arms of England since Alfred the Great bore the chequered scarlet and gold.

The following armorial bearings have also been adopted at various times, but in no case have they been established for any length of time.

3. Azure a fesse componce sable and or, a mullet pierced in the dexter, argent.

4. Azure fesse chequey or and sable in the first quarter, a mullet argent.

5. A difference has occurred in the Norfolk device given above : Azure a fesse paly of six gules and vert, between three owls argent.

6. Another branch is said to have borne argent a crosslet gules.[1]

7. The branches of Hereward at Odiham, county Hants, also in county Salop, bear : Chequy or and azure on a bend gules, three eagles displayed with two heads argent. It is obvious that the eagle borne by the Teutonic family of Hereward is the German and not the Austrian eagle.

8. Sir R. Hereward, county Cambridge, temp. Edward I., *circa* 1280, bore chequy or and azure on a bend gules, three eagles displayed argent.

The chief residence of the Herwards, Harwards, and Herewards has been in the shires of Warwick, Worcester, and Norfolk. For several generations a branch has settled in Devonshire, of which the present representative is Major H. B. Harward, of the Warwickshire Regiment, and occasional settlement has been made for short periods in the counties of Salop, Stafford, Berks, Hants, Middlesex, Surrey, Sussex, Gloucester, and Cornwall, but none of these have taken deep root.

[1] There is no proof that any Hereward went on Crusade, the only reference to it being contained in Sir Walter Scott's romance of "Robert of Paris," in which a Hereward is represented as commander of the Varangian Guard at Constantinople under Alexis Comnenus. The commandant was called "Acoulonthos," an acolyte or follower. Selected for bravery and trustworthiness, he was always in personal attendance upon the Emperor. The history of the Herewards in the twelfth century is difficult to trace.

The Evidence of the Heralds. 71

9. The Devon branch has flourished in that county for about two hundred years. It was lately represented by the Rev. Charles Harward, M.A., Dean of Exeter Cathedral, of Hayne House, near that city. His family had adopted a coat of arms varying in every respect from that of their ancestors.

Gules on a cross crosslet argent, between four guttes d'eau five annulets azure. Crest, a leopard statant erm., collared or, surmounting a cross fitchée sable, from the collar a chain or, reflexed and attached to the cross.[1]

The Norfolk branch of the family flourished for about five hundred years after the death of the hero of Ely, from the end of the eleventh century until the reign of Edward VI., when, on failure of lineal heirs male, the estates in the eastern counties devolved upon Thomas, second son of Hamond Claxton, Esq., of Great Livermore and Chesten, county Suffolk, through his wife Catherine, sole daughter and heiress of John Hereward, of Pensthorpe and Booton Hall. In the previous generation the Claxtons had intermarried with the Throckmortons.

The Norfolk branch of Hereward held a good landed estate in that county, and numerous generations are referred to in the county histories. Before they acquired their freehold estates, they held lands under Roger Bigot and Mowbray, Earls of Norfolk, who were tenants *in capite*.

Another original coat of arms was adopted by a very ancient branch of the family, which settled at Merrow, two miles from Guildford, in Surrey, not far distant from the original Hereward settlement at Horley, where the old castle of Thunderfield, and the manor still called Herewardislea, passed from the Herewards to the Abbot of Chertsey Monastery, and thence to Christ's Hospital.

[1] As no Hereward is known to have joined the Crusades, it is probable this coat is derived from collateral kindred or by marriage. It is emblematic of a crusader's history. During five years (annulets) he suffered much from intense heat and scarcity of water, as typified by only four drops of water. The crest shows he was captive, the leopard his English origin; he was held by a golden chain attached to the cross, indicating the price of his ransom or the Sacrifice of the Cross. There is no doubt the bearer remained a Christian during his captivity.

The Merrow branch flourished during the wars of the Roses, and bore in their fanciful shield the red rose of Lancaster. As stated above, they took little interest in the contest, but their sympathies were more on the Lancaster side, the widow of Henry V. having married a descendant of Griffith, King of North Wales, who married a daughter of Alfgar, Earl of Mercia.

The coat borne at Merrow was as follows :

10. Azure a lion rampant, over all on a fesse three roses gules. Crest, a demi-stag, ducally gorged and attired.

The old church at Merrow, built by the Herewards, and a good specimen of Saxon architecture, was lately pulled down to make way for a builder's edifice more in accord with the "progressive" taste of the modern lords of Merrow.

Amongst the most ancient memorials of the family, still in excellent preservation, are the brasses in the chancels of the churches of St. Cross, Winchester, Hants, and Boton, Norfolk. The date of that at St. Cross is 1493. It is in memory of Richard Harward, D.D., Warden of St. Cross.[1] The inscription is as follows: "Orate pro anima Magestri Ricardi Harward decretorum doctoris ac nuper hunc hospitalis Magistri qui obiit . . . die Aprilis Anno domini M.C.C.C.C. nonogesimo tertio. Cujus animæ propicietur Deus." Many words are abbreviated. Above the inscription is a full length figure of the doctor in the robes befitting his rank. The dress prescribed by Henry V. for doctors was "a violet gown pinfled with miniver." Knights of the Bath were ordered to be robed "like doctors." The long robe on the figure is trimmed with fur, and apparently the tails of sable. Biretta and stole are both worn. The hands are together raised in prayer. The brass, which is in good condition, is placed under a side table on the left-hand side of the chancel.

The brass in Boton Church has, unfortunately, no date upon it, but from the inscription is probably almost co-eval with that at St. Cross. It commemorates John Herward,[2] of

---

[1] See Appendix : Richard Harward, D.D., Warden of St. Cross.

[2] In Norfolk registers the name is variously spelt Hereward, Herward, and Harward.

The Evidence of the Heralds.

Boton Hall,[1] Norfolk, who died in 1568. His arms on the north wall of Boton Church are : A fesse gobonné argent and gules, between three owls of the second.

The inscription on the brass is " Orate pro anīma Johanni Herward qui obiit xvi. die Aprilis cujus animæ propicietur Deus. Amen." On this monument the year is altogether omitted, and in that at St. Cross the day of the month of decease is not recorded.

One small branch of the family only has extended to the northward of ancient Mercia as far as Derbyshire. An incomplete sketch pedigree of it will be found in the Appendix. It was lately represented by the Rev. John Harward, Vicar of Wirksworth. The device in arms borne by this offshoot of Hereward differs from that of all other Harwards, and completes the series ; it is as follows :

11. Argent, on a chevron gules two mullets of the field ; in chief two crescents azure ; in base a sinister hand couped and pierced, gules. Crest, a crescent argent. Motto, " In Deo salus."

We cannot conclude this notice without an expression of regret, on account of the evil which has been done in removing old landmarks and historical antiquities, whether in ancient churches, abbey ruins, or picturesque cottages, to make way for "something modern," and more in accordance with " the progressive views of this enlightened age."

Such vandalism is much to be deplored, and the matter is deserving of thought and action by all truly educated persons.

Archæological, scientific, and county field-societies can do much, and leading journals of non-destructive politics should

[1] In 1797 Boton Hall belonged to Mr. Peter Elwyn, born 1730, a descendant of the daughter and heiress of Anthony Rolfe, of Tuttington, whose ancestor Thomas married Pocahontas in Virginia, U.S.A. Her picture is at Boton Hall, and has around it the words, " Matoaka Rebecka filia potentiss. Princ. Powhatani Imp. Virginiæ." On a space beneath, "Matoaka als. Rebecka, daughter to the mighty prince Powhatano, Emperor of Attanoughkomouck als. Virginia, converted and baptized in the Christian faith, and wife to the Worsh[ll] Mr. Thomas Rolfe, Ætatis suæ 21, A. 1616." Pocahontas saved the lives of Sir Edward Smith, Governor, and the settlers at James Town, Virginia.

support archæological investigations more than they do, and raise their voice in behalf of historical truth.

One undoubted reason for this savage desire for destruction is the ostentatious vulgarism of modern buildings, whether in the style of Queen Anne, Italian, Romanesque, or pinchbeck timber-framed. They cannot bear comparison in point of taste or comfort with the old halls—now, perhaps, farmhouses —built four hundred years ago, and modern churches are generally an eyesore in the landscape.

This century has been an age of so-called progress and destructions; of jerry-builders and of mammon worshippers. May the next look to moderation and sound construction, and imitate the examples of ancient models, and preserve all the relics of antiquity that time has spared.

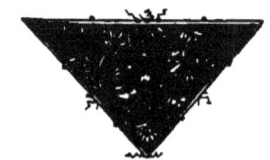

Chapter ix.

Descriptive of the Herewards after the Norman Conquest.

"My thoughts are with the dead ; with them
I live in long-past years,
Their virtues love, their faults condemn,
Partake their hopes and fears,
And from their lessons seek and find
Instruction with an humble mind."
ROBERT SOUTHEY—*The Scholar.*

"It would bore you to death should I pause to describe
Or enumerate half of the Hereward tribe
Who filled the background, and among whom were found
The *élite* of the old country families round."
Ingoldsby Legends (one word changed).

THE benefit derived by the English people from the marriage of Henry I. with the heiress of Edgar Atheling, uniting the Norman and Saxon lines, was almost neutralized by Stephen's imprudence and incapacity.

The few Saxon families still attempting to hold their own were mercilessly persecuted and plundered by the robber-chiefs enriched by William at the expense of the Saxons, and the swarms of foreign hirelings who pestered the country during the turbulent reign of Stephen. It was therefore a glad sign to the Old English when Henry II. (Curtmantle)[1] proved himself a new broom,[2] and not only made a clean sweep of the foreigners, but kept the Norman robber-barons in check.

The Herewards had fared badly under the Conqueror, but worse under his successors. The estates recorded in Domesday adjacent to the royal demesne at Coleshill, Warwickshire, had passed away, but they had acquired some lands at Bedworth (Pebwith), in Warwickshire, adjacent to Hereward's old estate of Marston Jabet, five miles from Nuneaton,[3] and also at Terrington and Aldborough, in Norfolk, and were settled in that county in Henry Plantagenet's reign, as shown by the grant of land to the church of Lynn. Though descended from royal kin, they held only the position of Franklins, but were marked, then and since, by a spirit of independence which no powerful neighbour could subdue, and no intrigue could beguile. Many an anxious year must they have spent watching their unscrupulous over-lords, and many a blow must they have struck in defence of their homesteads and dependants.

The jealousy and antagonism existing since the days of Edward the Confessor between the two hostile races of Normans and Saxons, aggravated by persistent misgovernment and feudal despotism, were almost at their height when Lion-hearted Richard succeeded his father, and the position of the Saxon gentlemen must have been almost intolerable under the perjured and profligate King John.

Wise counsels continued to prevail in the Hall of the Herewards at Terrington, or Bultees, and in 1302 Robert of Bultees, called also Herewards, was picked out for High Sheriff of Norfolk, and his great-grandson, Clement, named, no doubt, from the church of the Manor of Terrington, still known as St. Clement's, was elected a Knight of the Shire for

---

[1] It was a jest with the Normans, who were almost without exception men of low degree, that the Saxons had pedigrees as long as their cloaks. Henry II. introduced the short cloak, which fashion lasted nearly six hundred years. He was nicknamed "Curtmantle."

[2] The *planta-genista* was his device.

[3] See Domesday Book. To this day there are estates near Coleshill called Hereward Hall, Herewards, etc. Hereward had probably declined to hold land as a sub tenant under Bellamonte, Earl of Mellent.

The Herewards after the Conquest. 77

his county. Supported, as they must have been, by the Saxon peasantry, who still looked up to them as their national chiefs and lords, their estates had flourished, and, avoiding all strongly-marked political action, they devoted themselves to their own affairs and to the welfare of their own people. From the twelfth to the sixteenth centuries Herewards, Herwards, or Harwards, had held the manors of Aldborough, Terrington, Bultees or Herewards, Suffield, Cromer, Redeham, Gressinghall, Wykemere, Bowton, Great Bettering, Bolely, etc., and legacies were left to the poor of Norwich, Yarmouth, Cromer, South Repps, Suffield, Gunton, Antringham, Thorpe Market, Hanworth, Alby, Colby, and Aldeburgh (in all of which they must have had an interest) by Gregory Harwarde, of Redeham, Norfolk, in a will dated June 9, 6 Edward VI., 1552. A new and profitable industry in wool[1] had sprung up, and proved of more interest to the Hereward family than the twelve battles of the Roses during the Barons' Wars. The Barons—all of Norman origin —had done nothing but injury to the Herewards and their race, and it was extremely improbable that they would raise a finger in support of the internecine quarrel between the houses of York and Lancaster, for this was not a war where the interests of the people were concerned in the slightest degree.[2]

A branch of the Herewards, settled at Merrow, in Surrey, probably joined the standard of Henry VI., as they adopted the device of the Lancastrians,[3] and the three red roses in chief are still worn in their escutcheon.

The prudence of a tentative policy was justified by the

[1] At Crecy King Henry V. was called in derision "The English wool-merchant."

[2] The cause of this unholy war was the jealousy of the Norman robber-lords of one another, the decay of the feudal system, which had become intolerable to the people, the absence of a law of primogeniture, causing confusion in inheritance to the throne as well as to private estates. The people recovered their freedom through the Wars of the Roses; the Herewards were approving spectators of the contest.

[3] The estates of the Earl of Mellent, the Norman over-lord to Hereward, had devolved upon the Duke of Lancaster, who had also absorbed all other lands formerly belonging to the Earl of Mercia. See Appendix: "Duchy of Lancaster."

result, for Blomefield, the historian of the county of Norfolk, tells us that the family preserved a good estate in that county throughout the Barons' Wars, until, owing to failure of heirs male, the estates of the Norfolk branch passed to the Hamond-Claxtons of Suffolk, and the male line was continued in the Warwickshire line[1] through Richard Hereward, who shortly before this period married Elizabeth Greville, of a well-known family in that county, and founders of the noble house of the Earls of Warwick.

Before touching upon the changes which took place in both the estates and name of the family in the sixteenth century, we must premise that younger sons of the family had to be provided for, and branches and offshoots found their way into Berks, Hants and Devon, in the south, whilst other counties as far as London were visited, but no permanent settlement was formed or estate acquired except in Gloucestershire and Worcestershire, where lands are still held by the family.

The marriage of Richard Hereward, spelled erroneously "Hareward" in the Heralds' College Pedigree, with a carefully-designed object, no doubt, is not included in the pedigree of that family given in Dugdale's "History of Warwickshire," as it must have taken place in the early days of Henry VI., if not in the preceding reign. The lady he married, Elizabeth Greville, was most probably a daughter of John Greville, Sheriff of Glamorganshire, eldest son of William of Milcote, the founder of the Earl of Warwick's family. After the marriage the old Danish spelling of Harward was adopted, being more in accordance with the new English which had lately come into vogue,[2] and Hereward has not been so spelt since that time by any member of the family.

Two generations later we find the Harwards settled at Milcote, near Weston, on the Avon, on the borders of Gloucestershire and Warwickshire, until (so tradition goes) an alleged feud, or quarrel about land, induced the Harwards to

[1] See Heralds' Visitation, co. Warwick, 1619; Harleian Publications, vol. xii.

[2] In the new English Derby was pronounced and often spelt "Darby," and Herward would naturally be "Harward." It was, however, an ancient form of the name, and is found so spelled in the Norfolk registers.

The Herewards after the Conquest. 79

settle permanently at Hereforton,[1] ten miles from Evesham, and at Hartlebury, in Worcestershire.

About 1540 Thomas, whose father Richard had settled at Hartlebury, co. Wigorn, and married Joane, daughter of Richard Hollyns, married Joan Nashe, believed to be an aunt of Thomas Nashe, the husband of Shakespeare's granddaughter, Elizabeth, daughter of Susannah and Dr. Hall.

This Thomas, who represented the elder branch of the family, gave his eldest son, Francis, a university education, and he settled in London as a proctor in the Court of Arches. His second son, John, was appointed by Queen Elizabeth first of twenty-four feoffees, selected from the principal persons in the neighbourhood, to control the endowment of the Grammar School. The fourth feoffee was his younger brother Anthony, also of Hartlebury, whose son John, in default of heirs male of his uncles Francis and John, became the head of the family. He was much respected, and the eldest sons in eight out of the succeeding nine generations were named John. His descendant, John, who died in 1759, left two sons, of whom the elder, Samuel, acquired a valuable estate at Cheltenham, co. Gloucester. During the depression of that healthy and fashionable town a good deal of the land was sold in order to add to the estates in Worcestershire and Staffordshire, and the site was given on which the Queen's Hotel now stands. Samuel died without issue, and his estate devolved upon the two sons of his brother Michael, the Rev. John Harward, M.A., of Hartlebury, Rector of Icomb, Oxfordshire, and the Rev. Thos. Harward, M.A., of Winterfold, Worcestershire, and Rector of Rushock, both fellows of Worcester College, Oxon. The present family are the grandsons of the Rev. John Harward, and sons respectively of the Rev. J. Netherton Harward, M.A., and Thomas Netherton Harward, Esq., Barrister-at-law; their brothers, Major George Netherton Harward, 59th Regiment, and Samuel Netherton Harward, Esq., having died without issue, the latter unmarried.

It will be observed that the later seventeen generations

[1] See under Hereforton in "Collections for the History of Worcestershire," by T. Nash. "Several of the Harwards are interred in the body of the church."

are all descendants of Richard Hereward, or Harward, and Elizabeth Greville. Allusion has been made to a marriage with the Le Palmeres, of Francton, Warwickshire. John Hereward married Katherine, only daughter and heiress of Thomas Palmer, of Francton, co. Warwick,[1] and having succeeded to the advowson of the church of Francton in the reign of Henry VI., he twice instituted, jointly with his wife, incumbents to that living in the years 1427 and 1451.

There is no record of any issue of this marriage, and we have no further details of the history of this offshoot of the Herewards, or of the descendants of Le Palmere. The name is well known in Warwickshire, and a collateral representation of the family may be found in the line of the Rev. C. Palmer, of Ladbroke,[2] co. Warwick, who married January 23, 1823, Lady Charlotte, god-daughter of King George IV., and daughter of Heneage Finch, fourth Earl of Aylesford, of Packington Hall, Coventry, in the county of Warwick.

[1] Descended from Will. Le Palmere. See Appendix : " Hereward of Franckton, co. Warwick."

[2] An estate of Hereward's recorded in Domesday.

Chapter x.

Genealogical Outline.

"I come to thee for charitable license
To booke our dead."
SHAKESPEARE—*Henry V.*, iv. 7.

"Voices of the dead, not lost,
But speaking from Death's frost
Like fiery tongues at Pentecost."
LONGFELLOW.

ERHAPS the least interesting though most important records in the Bible, as well as in our secular histories, are the chapters containing genealogical tables. Originally the monks, and more recently those "learned in the law," and well acquainted with the value of the information contained in an accurate "family tree," have been the chief depositories of this most valuable knowledge, and it is astonishing to find this branch of research not only neglected, but absolutely repudiated by many persons who are well aware that the law does not allow any heir to obtain possession of his rightful estate without full proof of his identity and relationship to his ancestor.

Some worthy persons even go to the extent of renouncing the doctrine of heredity *in toto*, although it is clear that so long as the lower orders of creation are distinguished by their hereditary attributes and characteristics, we have the best argument, *à fortiori*, that distinctive marks of family will be transmitted throughout the generations of man.

In consideration, however, of the dryness of the subject, we propose to relegate our genealogies to the Appendix, merely noticing for immediate reference a bare outline of Herewards, Herwards and Harwards, tracing the stock from known sources through the descendants of Leofric, and the Herewards of Norman and Plantagenet days, to the Harwards of the Tudor and subsequent periods.

These key tables, like the ancient monastic records, will show only the heads of families, the stock from which derived, and the county in which located, with such dates or references to evidence as may be necessary for identification.

The Earls anterior to the Norman Conquest are recorded only in their proper names, as was then the custom throughout Europe, and is still the form in describing our own sovereigns.

Her Majesty is not known as Queen Guelph, but as Queen Victoria; and so in the early centuries the Herewards were known as Alfgar, Leofwine, and Leofric, until we come to the hero of these pages, who held no earldom, and was known only by the family name of Hereward.

The evidence afforded by the lands in Surrey, Sussex, and Oxfordshire, to which the Herewards gave their name, is sufficient proof that the family of this name were leaders of the Saxons in England at least as far back as the time of Ethelbald, King of Mercia, and most probably the lands were named after Hereward at the first foundation of the South Saxon kingdom about the end of the fifth century.

The direct descent of Hereward from the noble Earls of Mercia, including the Earldoms of Chester, Leicester, Lincoln, Hereford, and East Anglia, must be traced from his birthplace at Bourne, which is shown in Domesday to have become the property of Morcar, grandson of Leofric, Earl of Mercia, and the same indisputable authority proves that Hereward held lands in Warwickshire and Lincolnshire, which were at one time the property of Alfgar III., his reputed brother, and of Edwin, elder son of Alfgar, Hereward's nephew. To any reasonable mind this evidence must be conclusive as to the consanguinity of Hereward with the family of the last Earls of Mercia. It is the combined effect of this evidence, not in one instance only, but in three corroborating links, which affords the strongest confirmation of the assumption; and while the connection in estates in one instance might have been only a coincidence, the three distinct cases point distinctly and incontrovertibly to the fact of a family relationship. Evidence has also been given as to the relationship of Leofric and Alfgar to Ralph, Earl of Hereford, and through him to the reigning house of England, and there appears no reason to dispute this fact, or to doubt the kinship of the Mercian Earls to Edward the Confessor.

In the subsequent steps taken to evolve this genealogical sketch the following sources have been largely drawn upon :

1. The records of Domesday Book.
2. The Harleian MSS.
3. The Heralds' Visitations.
4. General and county histories.
5. Palgrave's "Saxon Commonwealth."
6. Various charters and deeds.
7. Local authorities on the heraldry of Worcestershire, Warwickshire, and Norfolk.
8. Pedigree drawn out by the late Sir T. Phillips, F.S.A., a trustee of the British Museum, for the Rev. J. Harward, M.A., of Hartlebury.
9. Monastic records.
10. Manuscripts and seals in the British Museum.

In no sense has any exhaustive search been yet made to prove the earlier steps of this pedigree ; but the writer feels assured that historical documents will yet be found to amplify and strengthen the facts already known, and that patient inquiry and investigation will be amply rewarded. As stated in an earlier part of this work, the present memoir has been drawn up as an initial base upon which an interesting work can be raised. At present many points are still open to discussion upon which further effort is invited and required, until the work is completed.

Before proceeding to enumerate the antecessors of Hereward, the Saxon hero, we must briefly glance at the changes which had taken place in the Anglo-Saxon community, and affected the Hereward family. Established in the heart of the Mercian kingdom, with rank second only to that of their provincial King, they must have early felt the effect of the landing of the Danes near Grimsby, and their aggression in East Anglia; and it is probable that, true to their Scandinavian origin, they were inclined to look upon the Danes rather as friends than foes, and, although many a hard fight took place between the Saxons and their Danish cousins, in one of which, at Strekingham, in Kesteven, Lincolnshire, Alfgar II., great-grandfather of Leofric III., the great Earl of Mercia, was slain, the two tribes easily coalesced when the Danes abandoned the worship of Thor and Woden and were admitted within the pale of the Christian Church. There was little difference between the Anglo-Dane and the Anglo-Saxon. The religious difficulty appears to have been at the root of the enmity which existed between the pagan Danes of the north and the Saxons in England who had embraced the Christian faith.

The marriage of Ethelwulf, father of Alfred the Great, to Osburga, daughter of Oslac, his Danish cup-bearer, and ancestor of Duke Oslac in Edgar's reign, who was related to Hereward's mother, was an event of great importance, and the precursor of many similar marriages between Saxon and Danish families. There is evidence to show that the Herewards were as friendly with Dane as with Saxon, and it was by the partiality of King Canute that Leofric III. obtained the earldom of the entire province of Mercia.

At this period the rank of ealdorman, answering to that of Roman curule magistrate, borne by the Saxon chiefs, was changed for that of earl, the Danish title. Alfred was the first nobleman mentioned in history upon whom this rank was conferred, and although Leofric I., the ancestor of Hereward, is known in mediæval records as Earl of Leicester, he was probably styled at that period, A.D. 745, Ealdorman of Leicester, though his son Alfgar of Lincoln may have had the Danish rank of earl in A.D. 757-839. The custom of hereditary descent of titles at this time was for the son to inherit the rank of his father if of full age, and if the family influence and estate had been maintained ; but about A.D. 800 Hugh Capet, King of France, conferred an absolute hereditary right upon the feudal nobility to retain their rank. The ancient custom, however, prevailed in England until the Norman Conquest, and it appears that the position and influence of the family of Leofric increased considerably during the six generations anterior to the Norman Conquest.

The rank and pedigree of Leofric, Earl of Mercia *temp.* Edward the Confessor, assures us that for at least six generations an earldom was hereditary, although called "Chester," "Hereford," "Leicester," and finally "Mercia." Their territory may have been more limited in earlier days, and latterly their influence was far greater in extent and power. Mediæval records may yet yield further knowledge of the ancestors of Leofric, and of the families of Oscar and other Danish chiefs, who from the time of Alfred settled in the eastern counties, and who could only maintain their status in England by inter-marrying with the Anglo-Saxon nobles, who were, in fact, of the same Scandinavian origin.

Since the Wars of the Roses the powers of the English nobility have been much curtailed. As a class they are looked upon with jealousy by the people, many of the untitled being of older lineage and better blood than the late peers, who are constantly recruited from the ranks of the vulgar plutocracy.

Key to Genealogy of Hereward and Harward.

PEDIGREE IN OUTLINE OF THE HEREWARD FAMILY ANTERIOR TO THE NORMAN CONQUEST.

Hereward, the founder of the family in England, settled in Surrey, and afterwards in the Midland counties, about A.D. 600, and his descendant, Leofric I., was Earl of Leicester in the time of Ethelbald, King of Mercia, 745-757. His son, Alfgar I., was created Earl of Lincoln, 757-839, and lived in the reigns of Offa, Kenulph and Wiglaf, Kings of Mercia. He

was succeeded by his son Alfgar II. in the Earldom of Lincoln, who was killed in conflict with the Danes Ungar and Ubba at Strekingham, in Kesteven, Lincolnshire.[1] He was buried with his fathers at Croyland Abbey, which they had assisted to endow. He lived in the time of the Mercian Kings Bernulf and Buhred (spelt "Burgred"), 839-872. His son Leofric II., 872-925, living in the reigns of Alfred and of his son Edward the Elder, was created Earl of Leicester, and succeeded by his son Leofwine, whose brothers were both killed, Edwin by the Welsh, and Northman, or Norman, by King Canute, together with Edric, Duke of Mercia, 925-975.

Leofric III., the great Earl of Mercia and son of Leofwine, the "noble founder of many abbeys," lived in the days of Edward II., Ethelred II., Canute, Harald, Hardicanute, and Edward III. (the Confessor), Kings of England. He was undoubtedly the Earl of Mercia, and one of the three powers which swayed the destinies of England. He was favoured by Canute,[2] owing doubtless to his marriage with Godgifu, or Godiva, a daughter of Thorold, Vicecomes of Lincoln, and connected with Duke Oslac. He lived to be nearly eighty years of age, from 975-1057, and was buried in the Abbey of Coventry, one of the many religious houses founded and supported by his munificence and charity. By his influence he raised Harold Harefoot to supreme power in England. In 1041 he assisted in the rough punishment awarded to the citizens of Worcester, and in 1047-1048 strenuously opposed the grant of fifty ships to Sweyne, which Earl Godwin advised, and three years later summoned his forces to the field in support of King Edward against Godwin, who

[1] The learned author of "Lincolnshire and the Danes," Bishop Trollope, and Mr. Kemble throw doubt upon the alleged battle at Strekingham or Threckingham. The last name is supposed to commemorate the death of three Danish leaders killed in the battle on the first day, when the Saxons prevailed. There can be no doubt that the expedition under Ubba and Ungar, or Hingvar, subjugated the whole of East Anglia; and that one of the principal battles was fought near this spot is testified by local tradition, corroborated by the "Danes' field" still existing. The record is supported by Danish writers, and rests upon more assured fact than many uncontroverted details of history.

[2] Palgrave (Cohen), proofs and illustrations to "The Saxon Commonwealth."

was equally treacherous and unscrupulous, and whose ambitious schemes were ingloriously closed by the death of his son Harold at the Battle of Hastings.

Leofric's son, Alfgar III., Earl of East Anglia, and afterwards Earl of Mercia, had suffered a decree of outlawry by the machinations of Godwin, and fled to Wales, from which province he soon returned, and with the aid of Gruffydd, King of North Wales,[1] who married his sister, he recovered his earldom, and eventually succeeded to all his father's honours and territory. He was father of Edwin, created Earl of Warwick, and, on his father's death, Earl of Mercia; and of Morcar, made Earl of Northumberland; the former was slain in an ambush, and Morcar surrendered at Ely, and was imprisoned for life by William. The estates and honours of both Edwin and Morcar fell to their sister Lucia,[2] married by William's order to Ivo de Taillebois. It is probable there were younger sons of one or more of these chiefs besides Leofric III., but the pedigree drawn out by the abbey monks was intended only for the benefit of the elder branch, and cadets were rigorously excluded from mention; and from this cause so little is known directly of Hereward's relationship to Leofric and his family, though collateral evidence is strong in proof of his consanguinity to the royal family of England, both in the lands held by him in Warwickshire, his alleged burial at Croyland with Leofric's family; his home at Bourne, in Lincolnshire, recorded in Domesday as belonging to Morcar, upon whom it had probably been settled by his father Alfgar, who as Earl of Mercia had numerous estates at his disposal. Hereward's alleged roughness with other youths must have been at Court.[3] In village life such a matter would certainly not have come before the King, and would, in fact, have been merely looked upon as horseplay. I fail to see any other origin of the Hereward family, and do not hesitate to place Hereward in the pedigree as one of the brothers of Alfgar, thus:

[1] From whose daughter descended Llewelyn, last Prince of North Wales and ancestor of Sir Owen Tudor, grandfather of Henry VII.
[2] See Appendix: "Lucia."
[3] Appendix: "Hereward's Parentage." Also Chapter III.

(A) DIRECT LINE TO THE NORMAN CONQUEST.

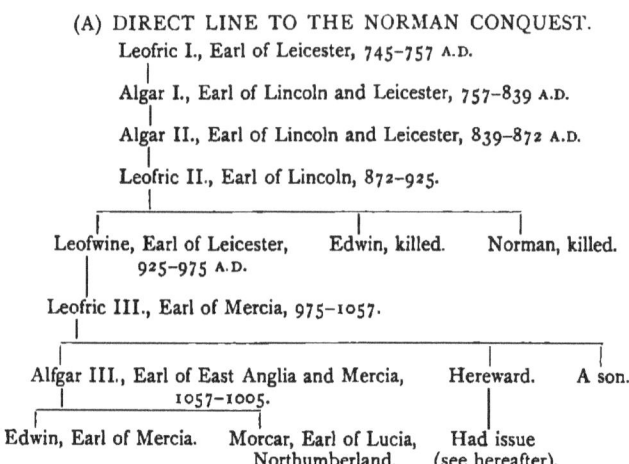

Five of the six first Earls of this line have names with a distinct Danish termination, "ric" or "gar," and it is not too much to suppose that the family, of Saxon origin, had consistently intermarried with Danes, which obtained for them the goodwill of Osburga, wife of Ethelwulf, and of her father Oslac, and, later on, of the powerful Duke Oslac and of the King Canute. Leofric's wife, Godiva, is said to have been a daughter of Thorold, Vicecomes (Sheriff) of Lincoln, and a connection of Duke Oslac. Of the wives of the other Earls there is unfortunately no record, but traces of them may yet be found.

Hereward, the renowned, appears, then, to be of Saxon descent modified by Danish alliances, and as both were of the same origin, he can only be described as Anglo-Saxon. He is said to have married twice, but there is no record of his family by his second wife, Alfryth, until the time of Henry II., and except that his only daughter by his first wife, Torfrida, married a Norman lord, Hugh de Evermue, of Deeping, Lincolnshire, we have no knowledge of his descendants for a hundred years, when two families are found in Warwickshire and Norfolk bearing the name of Hereward, but the connection with the Saxon hero is completely established by the record of the "Historia Ecclesiæ Eliensis," that Hereward, husband of Wilburga, of Terrington (Taunton), Norfolk, in the reign of Henry II., 1155-85, granted a carucate of land in Torrington to the church at Len (Lynn), and directed that prayers should be said for the souls of Hereward, his father, and of Hereward, "the exile," his grandfather. The date of the latter's death is uncertain, but the three generations are completely established, and Hereward must have left male issue, probably more than one son, as Herewards were established at Pebwith,[1] in Warwickshire, as well as in Norfolk in the time of Henry III. The Visitation of Warwickshire gives the following sketch of that branch to about 1460:

(B) WARWICKSHIRE BRANCH PEDIGREE.

FROM HERALDS' VISITATION, 1619; HARLEIAN PUBLICATIONS, vol. xii.

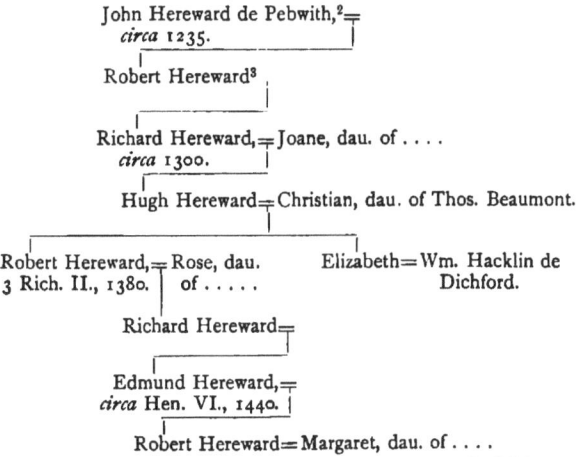

[1] Heralds' Visitation of Warwickshire, 1619. Harleian Library, vol. xii. Pebwith became Pebworth and Bedworth.

[2] Presumably Pebworth, or Bedworth, near to Marston Jabet, one of Hereward's estates in Domesday.

[3] An ancient deed in the Record Office, "Warwick, B. 390," describes a grant of land by Hereward (Richard, 1300), son of Robert de Bedeworthe.

The name and fame of the great Hereward must have been so well established in Warwickshire, where Hereward had estates since the time of Edward the Confessor, that there is reason to suppose the elder branch may have settled in that county, and it was certainly the Warwickshire branch that afterwards settled at Hartlebury, co. Worcester. In 1200 the Norfolk and Warwick branches must have been very closely related.

The Herewards remained in Warwickshire until the sixteenth century, when that branch—the Norfolk line having become extinct—settled at Hartlebury and Harvington (Hereforton), co. Worcester.

The Norfolk branch presents a fairly clear succession of Herewards, Herwards, and Harwards. The record of the great book of the Church of Ely, "Liber Ecclesiæ Eliensis," and the registers of Aldborough (St. Mary's) and St. Clement's, Terrington, as well as of Boton, contain many entries, and copies of numerous wills of members of the family are extant. Theobald de Hereward, and William, his son, held Aldeburgh under Earl Roger Bigot.[1] Robert Hereward was a witness to deeds sans date, and was living in 1376. In 4 Henry IV. the heirs of Robert Hereward held it of Lord Mowbray, Duke of Norfolk. Robert Hereward was Sheriff of Norfolk 1302, and Sir John Howard, the ancestor of the present Duke of Norfolk, was Sheriff forty-three years afterwards, proving there were Herewards and Howards, and that the Herewards at that time had prior claims to social distinction, and that the names were not interchangeable, as the "Peerage" notice would have us believe. This branch flourished from the Norman Conquest to the beginning of the seventeenth century.

The Norfolk branch became extinct in the early part of the seventeenth century, on the marriage of Catherine, only

---

A later deed, B. 407, records a grant of land by William Hereward of Bedeworth on Christmas Eve, 12 Richard II. Hereward was therefore lord of Bedworth, misspelt by the Heralds "Pebwith."

[1] Earl Bigot only held his manors in Norfolk for five generations from the Conquest, and Theobald and William both held under him; so both these Herewards must have been within the five generations.

daughter and heiress of John Hereward, of Pensthorpe, with Thomas, second son of Hamond Claxton, Esq., of Great Livermore and Cheston, in the county of Suffolk, to whom the Norfolk estates of the Herewards descended in default of heirs male, and we must return to the Warwickshire branch, of which the meagre outline in the Heralds' Visitation of 1619 is given above. In this outline the eldest sons only are recorded, but with the dates and places of settlement on record, it is not difficult to connect the relationship of the younger sons in Warwickshire.

Reverting to the Warwickshire branch pedigree, we find two families of Hereward in the county of Warwick in the reign of Richard II., and while there is indisputable proof that Robert was the elder son of Hugh, there is also ample evidence that Richard was his younger son, and his great-grandson, also Richard, left Milcote, on the banks of the Avon, for the richer lands of the Severn Valley at Hartlebury:

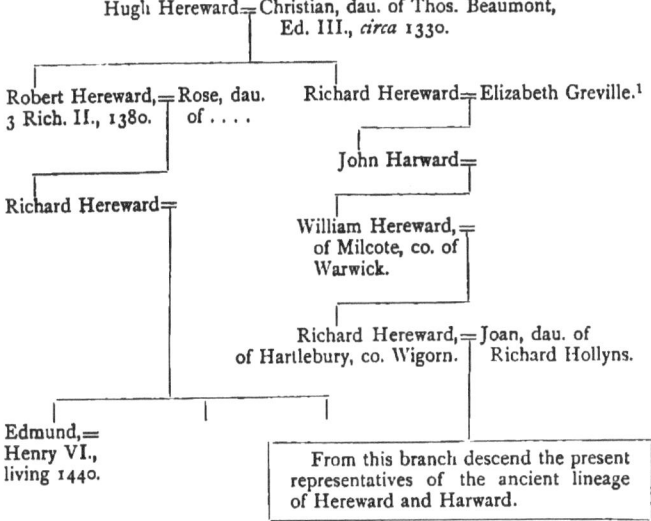

[1] In 1398 William Greville, a citizen of London, and founder of the family of the present Earl of Warwick, purchased the Manor of Milcote, co. Warwick, where the Herewards also resided until they moved to Hartlebury.

(C) SKETCH PEDIGREE OF ROUMARA OF REVESBY,

SHOWING FAMILY OF THE COUNTESS LUCIA, DAUGHTER OF EARL ALFGAR, AND MARRIAGE OF HER DESCENDANT WITH SIR GILBERT, OR GILLIBERT, EARL OF GHENT OR GANT.

```
           Albreda=Gerold Roumara,=Amicia.
                    temp. Will. I.
                         |
           Roger=Countess Lucia¹,=Ralph, Earl of Chester.
                   | dau. of Earl
                     Alfgar.
                         |
              William, Earl of Lincoln,=
           1142, founded Cistercian Abbey
           of Clyve, or Cliffe, co. Somerset,
                  temp. Stephen.
                                    |
                         Rohais,=Gillebert of Gant, became Earl of
  dau. and heiress of William      Lincoln in right of his wife
  (see Catalogue of Seals, British  Rohais; assumed the name of
  Museum); Countess of Lincoln.    Lucia, Lacie, or Lacy, and had
                                    issue.
```

---

[1] It is said that the Countess was first married, or betrothed, probably while a ward of the Crown, to Ivo de Taillebois, Lord of Spalding. If this is correct she had three husbands, as generally alleged.

The genealogy of the husbands of the Countess Lucia and their descendants shows some confusion in dates, as recorded in Dugdale's "Monasticon," which has been utilized by the manufacturers of Norman pedigrees to prove that "the whole story of Lucia, daughter of Earl Alfgar, is a myth!" Inaccuracy in dates is characteristic of most ancient documents and fair proof of their genuine origin. Absolute proof of the relationship here given will be found in the Record Office Deeds, 69 S.D., 69a S.D., in the Appendix to 35th Report of the Deputy Keeper of the Public Records.

Genealogical Outline.

(11) KEY TABLE OF THREE BRANCHES OF THE FAMILY OF HEREWARD OR HARWARD.

Torfryth, of Bruges, =Hereward, of Mercia=Ælfthryth, a ward of Bishop Wulfstan.
Flanders.
|
Torfrida=Hugh de Evermue.

Hereward, son of the above, referred to in "The Great Book of Ely."
|
Hereward,=Wilburga, of Terrington, co. Norfolk.
grandson of the above, bequeathed land to church of Lynn, Norfolk, for prayers for himself, his father, and his grandfather, "the exile."
|
— John Hereward, of Pebwith, or Bedworth, co. Warwick.
— Theobald de Hereward had Aldeburg, or Aldburgh, under Earl Roger Bigot.
    |
    William de Hereward of Aldeburgh, Norfolk.
    |
    Robert Hereward, Sheriff of Norfolk 1302, *temp.* Ed. I.
    |
    — Robt. Hereward,=Widow held Bultees 1401.
      of Bultees, *als.* Herewards, co. Norfolk.
    — Robt. Hereward,=Widow buried in St. Mary's, Aldborough.
      buried in St. John's Chapel, Aldborough, co. Norfolk.

A quo Hereward of Norfolk, whose large estates passed by marriage of Catherine, only dau. of John Hereward, who died 1568, to Hamond Claxton,[1] of Great Livermore and Cheston, co. Suffolk.

Richard Hereward,=Joane, dau. of
circa 1300, Ed. I. | .....
|
Hugh Hereward=Christian, dau. of Thos. Beaumont.
|
— Robert Hereward=Rose, dau. of
  (3 R. II. 1380). | .....
  |
  — Richd Hereward=
    |
    — Edmund, *temp.* H. B.
    — Richard, D.D., Warden of St. Cross, Winchester, *o.s.p.*
    — Robert,=Margaret.
      o.s.p.

The above Robert Hereward dying without issue, the eldest branch became extinct *circa* 1500 A.D.

Rich. Hereward=Elz. Greville. See Warwick, Earl of.
|
John Hereward, of Milcot, co. Warwick.
|
— John=Katherine le Palmer, of Frankton, co. Warwick, *o.s.p.*
— Willm Harward, of Milcot, co. Warwick.
  |
  Richd Harward,=Joan, dau. of of Hartlebury, co. Wigorn. | Rich. Hollyns.

A quo Harward of Worcestershire, elder surviving branch of Hereward.

[1] The ruins of Claxton Castle still remain in Norfolk.

93

(E) SKETCH PEDIGREE OF THE HEREWARDS IN NORFOLK.

TORFRYTH, or TORFRIDA = HEREWARD, the Saxon Patriot = ÆLFTHRYTH.

- **A daughter = Hugh de Evermue,** Lord of Deeping.
- **HEREWARD,** mentioned in "The Great Book of the Church of Ely," as father of the next Hereward, husband of Wilburga.
- **Theobald de HEREWARD** held *Aldburgh* under Earl Roger Bigot, and was succeeded by his son William (Blomefield's "History of Norfolk," vol. viii., p. 72).

- **HEREWARD, = Wilburga, dau. of ....** grandson, bequeathed one carucate of land in Terrington to the church of Len (Lynn), Norfolk. Terrington, *temp.* Henry II., 1154, 1189.
- **WILL de HEREWARD** witnessed deed sans date of SUNNOLF, father of Robert, 1st Mayor of Lynn, *circa*, 1284, 12 Ed. I.

ROBERT HEREWARD, b. *circa* 1260; High Sheriff of Norfolk 1302; ob. *circa* 1335.

- **ROBERT HEREWARD, = His widow held Bultees in 1401.** had the Manor called Bultees, *als.* Herewards, co. Norfolk; was living in 1376. It descended to Clem¹ in 1426, and to his son Robert.
- **ROB. HEREWARD,** probably a nephew of the Sheriff, Archdeacon of Taunton; a Commissioner to treat with the French before the Pope at Avignon, anno 1334, appointed by Edward III.

ROBERT HEREWARD, = Margaret, dau. of .... buried in St. Mary's, of Bultees and Aldborough; buried in St. John's Chapel, Aldborough. Aldborough.

CLEMENT HEREWARD, = Cecily, dau. of .... exe^trx of husband's will; had Manor of Wykmere. Bur^d St. Mary's, Aldbro'. of Aldborough and Bultees; M.P., 1386, for Norwich; ob. 1427; will did. 2nd Nov., 1426; provd. 24th Jany., 1427.

- **Mary, = Rob. of Aldborough,** d. of John Burney, of Redeham, by his wife Isabel, d. of Sir Jno. Heveringham. son, and had Manor 2nd Nov., 1426. Will 1483.
- **Amey, d. of Rob. Rands,** of Horsham, St. Faith's. Will 18th Dec., 1485; bur. at Aldbro'.
- **Thomas, = dau. of ....** had 2 sons living in 1426; also in 1452, N.
- **Margaret = Jno. Pagrave** Hereward, legatee for 100 marks. (Palgrave), of Berningham, his 1st wife living in 1426, *s.p.*

Margaret Alice, under 18.   Anne = M. Jno. le Gros, of Crosweight.

- **Clement = 1st wife,** of Aldbro', 1st son, d. 1509. d. of Lovell, of Harling, co. Norfolk.
- **= 2nd wife, Anna, d. of Astley, of Melton, Norfolk.**
- **4th son, = d. of ROB. of Booton, 4 sons bur. in Booton Church with 3 wives. Powlt (Powlton).**
- **Mary of Brampton, Suffolk, Esq.** d. of Thos., Duke,
- **d. of Gerney,** his 2nd wife, widow of Walter Garny, d. Ed. Moon, of Wilterton.
- **2nd son, = d. of JOHN HERWARD, of South Repps, gent., b. 1524.**
- **3rd son, Wooton. Richard, lived at Boton. Will 1547, F.31, Coode, P.C.C.**

Doucebell, sans issue, baptized 1543, June 17.

George. Thomas.

Gregory, will 1552; m. Eliz., d. of Jno. Burney, of Redeham, Esq., *o.s.p.*
John, lived 1552.¹ m. Engloys.
Dau. m. Broomfylde.
Dau. m. Becke.
Dau., Mary, m. Galte.
Dau. m. Bazely.
Joan, unm. 1552.

Thomas.

- **Thos., = Dau. of** eldest Bartson, lett, lived at *o.s.p.* Boton in 1549.
- **Jno., = Bridgett,** d. of Pensthorp, 2nd s. and h. of Boton, ob. 1568. d. of Christopher Perm, of West Barsham, in Norfolk.
- **Clemt., = Amy, d. of** of Tostrees, in Norfolk, lvg. 1558; m. 2nd, W. Grey, of Hempton. H. Clifton, Andrew, of Derham, gent.
- **Frances, Margory Quarly,** uxor. of Th. wich. of Nor = Jno. Berney, bap. 22, 11, 1588.
- **Henry,** will 1551, 5 Ed. VI. Clement, bap. Dec. 10, 1589.
- **Bridgett,** Anne, unmar. 1577. Henry, bap. Ap. 27, 1593.
- **The = Margaret Su-Ting,²** above Thomas Nov. 16, 1587, at Aldbro'. A daughter, bap. 5th Jany, 1594.

- **Robt., only son,** *o.s.p.* Had he lived would have inherited Boton and also Aldebury, under the will of his cousin Clement (1586).
- **Catherine, = Thomas, 2nd son of Hamond** only d. and h^s. Claxton, of Great Livermore, in Suffolk. Hamond was 2nd son of Will. Claxton and Eliz. Throckmorton, of Cheston, Suffolk.
- **Henry Herward,** of Aldeburgh, Will May 28th, 1577, *o.s.p.*
- **Clement Herward, = Eleanor,** of Alborow and Grisenhall. Had Aldby 1573. Will Nov. 15th, 1586, *o.s.p.* d. of ... buried Jan. 23rd, 1590, at Aldburgh.
- **Katherine** buried 19th July, Aldbro' 1590.

So Boton estate passed to the HAMOND-CLAXTONS, of Great Livermore and Cheston, co. Suffolk, and Hereward of Norfolk became extinct.

¹ Will of John of Poole, Dorset, 1588, F. 19, Noodes. Prerogative Court of Canterbury.
² Illegible in original.

This Pedigree is compiled chiefly from Blomefield's "History of Norfolk," Registers of Aldbro' and Boton, and several wills still extant.

(F) KEY TABLE OF HARWARD, OR HEREWARD, OF HARTLEBURY, CO. WIGORN, 1410 A.D. TO 1807 A.D.

Genealogical Outline.

```
RICHARD HEREWARD,[1] = Eliz[a] Grevil, or Greville, of Milcot, co. Warwick.
Cadet of John Hereward, | See "Peerage," Warwick, Earl of.
of Pebwith, co. Warwick. |
         |
    John Harward, of Milcot, co. Warwick = No record.
         |
    William Hereward, of Milcot = No record.
         |
    Richard Hereward, of Hartlebury = Joan, dau. of Rich[d] Hollyns.
         |
    Thomas Hereward, of Hartlebury = Joane Nashe.
         |
    ┌──────────────────────┬─────────────────────────────────┐
Francis, Proctor = Sibell, d. of Hugh    John Hereward[2], = Joan, dau. of John    Anne = Anthony Harward[3] = Margaret Hill.
of Court of Arches. Parry of Acombury.   or Harward, of Hartlebury,  Barnesley, of Bar-
                                         co. Wigorn, married 1550.  nesley Hall.
    │                                        │                                    ┌──────┬──────┬──────┬──────┐
William. Edmund. Robert, Thos.  Creature, Thomas. Charles, John.  Dorothy = John = Anne,  Rich., Edw[d], Emma, Francis, Humfry.
              1595.[4]           b. 1551; Margery. 1563. Cicely.  d. 1608.    dau. of   b. 1570. b. 1573. b. 1575. b. 1577.
                                  d. 1552. Jane.                              Jones.
                     ┌──────┐                    ┌──────┬──────┐                                        ┌──────────┐
                 John,  Margaret. Anthony Elinor. Simon. Joan.              John, = Thomas, = Martha.
                 b. 1583. Anne.                                              b. 1566. living 1607.
                                       │
                 ┌────┬────┬─────┬─────┴─┬──────┐
              Phillis. Mary. Urban. Anthony = Joan. James = Joan Glover. Thomas = Elizabeth, dau. of ....
                                                                Elizabeth.  b. 1709.  d. 1666.
                                       │
                                   ┌───┴───┬──────────┐
                                 Elinor.  Mary.  Elizabeth.  Margaret = Richard.
                                       │
                               Rev. Thomas, =
                                 b. 1659.
                                       │
                               Martin, Worcester Coll., Oxon.; M.A.,
                               1680; Vicar of Winterbown, Wilts, 1678
                               to 1708; Rector Rolleston, Wilts,
                               1708-21.
                                       │
                               MICHAEL OF HARTLEBURY, = m. 1759, Mary, dau. of Francis
                                 b. 1728; d. 1807.      Perrins, Esq.

    Margaret, = JOHN, = Margery
    dau. of ....  1619,  of Clent.
                  1677.
              │
        John, = Mary.
        b. 1649.│
           John, = No record.
           b. 1677.│
              Mary, = John, = Elizabeth.
              d. 1711. d. 1759.

    Edward =
         │
    Samuel of Cheltenham[5]
    co. Gloucester, o.s.p.
```

For descendants direct and collateral see Sketch Pedigree (G).

[1] See Key Table (D). [2] The first-named in a list of twenty-four gentlemen appointed trustees of Hartlebury Grammar School by Queen Elizabeth. Nash's "History of Worcestershire." [3] Appointed fourth in list of trustees of Grammar School. [4] *A quo descendit* Harward of Harvington. [5] Acquired a large estate, upon which a part of the town of Cheltenham is built.

(G) KEY TABLE OF MICHAEL HARWARD, Esq., OF HARTLEBURY, Co. WIGORN.

MICHAEL HARWARD, b. 1728; d. 1807. = Mary, dau. of Francis Perrins, Esq. of Hartlebury, d. 1807.

Children:

- **Rev. John**, of Hartlebury, b. 1760; d. 1855; M.A. Oxon. = **Susanna**, dau. of Thos. Sansom, Esq., of St. Margaret's, Westminster, niece of Sam. Netherton, Esq., High Sheriff, Worces., 1792. And has issue six sons and six daughters. See Key Table (I).

- **Charlotte**, s.p. **Jane**, s.p.

- **Mary**, b. 1761. = **Rev. Ed. Waldron**, Rector of Hampton Lovett, co. Worcester, son of Rev. J. Waldron, Rector of Elmley, co. Worcester.

- **Sarah**, b. 1767. = **Rev. Allan Wheeler**, The Close, Worcester, and has issue.

- **Susan** = **Rich. Gardiner**, Esq., of Bath, and has issue.

- **Rev. Thos.**, M.A. Oxon. = **Elizabeth**, dau. and heir of W. H. Wheeler, Esq., of Winter Fold Park, Chaddesley, Worcestershire.

Issue of Rev. John and Susanna (shown as next generation):

- **Mary Anne** = **George Lowther Thompson, Esq.**, J.P., D.L., of Sheriff-Hutton Castle, co. York.

- **Leonard**,[2] o.s.p. = **Lady Mary**, dau. of the Rt. Hon. Wm. Thos. Spencer Wentworth, Earl Fitzwilliam, Lord Lieutenant of the West Riding of co. York.

- **Edward**, Capt. 61st Regiment, o.s.p. = **Ann B. Garnett**, of Bromich House, Worc., m. 2ndly, Rev. T. L. Wheeler, M.A., Canon and Precentor Worc. Cath., son of Rev. Allan Wheeler. Has issue Ellen, o.s.p., and Rev. T. L. Wheeler, M.A.

- **John**, in Holy Orders. = **Mrs. Burt**, a widow.

- **Elizabeth Ann**,[1] b. 1814.

- **Augusta**,[1] b. 1815; d. 1868, s.p.

- **William**, b. 1816; d. 1892, s.p.

- **Elizabeth**,[1] m. 2ndly, Capt. Eyre Coote Lord, bro. of Sir J. Owen, Bart., of Orielton, co. Pembroke. Has issue a son, d. an infant, and three daus., Mrs. Bowyn, Mrs. Dr. Jones, and Mrs. Lord, who m. a cousin. = **Major Lewis**, E.I.C.S. Has issue John, Colonel 37th Regt, o.s.p., and Georgina, m. Rev. Rich[d] Lewis, D.D., Lord Bishop of Llandaff.

- **Mary Jane**,[1] b. 1817.

- **George** = **Elizabeth Lewis**, aunt of Rev. R. Lewis, D.D, Lord Bishop of Llandaff.

[1] These ladies have succeeded as tenants in common to their father's and brother's estates in Worcestershire, Staffordshire and Gloucestershire.

[2] On the death of Leonard Thompson without issue, Sheriff-Hutton Castle and the Yorkshire estate devolved upon his cousin.

Genealogical Outline.

(H) KEY TABLE OF HARWARD OF HARVINGTON, Co. WIGORN,
1595 A.D. TO 1750 A.D.

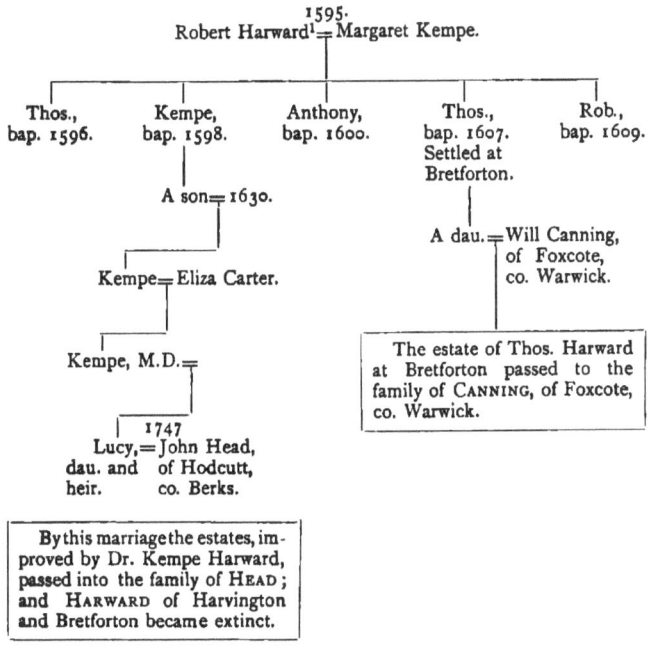

See Pedigree of Robert, third son of Francis, Proctor of the Court of Arches, eldest brother of John Hereward, or Harward, of Hartlebury, co. Wigorn.

(I) KEY TABLE OF THE REV. JOHN HARWARD, M.A., OF HARTLEBURY, Co. WIGORN.

Rev. JOHN HARWARD, M.A., = Susanna, dau. of Thos. Sansom, Esq., Queen's Messenger, of Bewdley, co. Wigorn, and St. Margaret's, Westminster; niece of Samuel Netherton, Esq., High Sheriff of Worcestershire, 1793.

Oxford; Fellow Worc. Coll., Oxon; Rector of Icomb, Oxon, 1795 to 1854; was born 1760; d. 1854, æt. 93.

Children:

- **Rev. Jno. Netherton Harward, M.A.**, Senr. Scholar, Worc. Coll., Oxon; b.1797; d. 1863; Matric. 1814; B.A. 1818; M.A. 1820; grand tour of Europe 1820 to 1823; Chaplain to Lord Bishop of Rochester; Vicar of Kemsing Cum Seal, Kent, and East Grinstead, Sussex. = **Harriet**, dau. of Rich. Butler, Esq., of West Hall, Cheltenham, d. 1894, and has issue.

- **Thos. Netherton Harward, E-q.**, Barrister-at-Law, Lincoln's Inn; Matric. Worc. Coll., Oxon, 1822; b. 1803; d. 1894, and has issue. = **Charlotte**, d. of R. Gardiner, Esq., of Bath.
  1. Ed. Netherton, b. 1838, m. 1893.
  2. Gainsborough, b. 1840, twice m., and has issue, John Donaldson, b. 1871.

  N.B.—Two sons and four daus. of the above Rev. J. Harward died in infancy.

- **Marianne**, b. 1800; d. 1889, and has issue. = **J. Griffiths, Esq., J.P., D.L., of the Weir, Herefordsh., bro. of E. Griffiths, Esq., J.P., D.L., Chairman Quarter Sessions of Newcourt, Hereford, and of Lewis Griffiths, Esq., M.P. for Cheltenham, of Marle Hill.

- **Caroline**, and has issue. = **Rev. A. J. B. Hooper, M.A., Rector of Upton Warren, Worc., and Rural Dean.

- **George** = **Sophia**, d. of J. Netherton, Hooper, Major Esq., of 59th Rose Foot, Bank, b. 1808; Worc. d. 1867, s.p.

- **Sam. Netherton Harward**, b. 1811; matric. Worc. Coll., Oxon, 1831; o.s.p. 1837.

Next generation:

- **John, Lieut. R.N., b. 1824; issue. d. 1854, s.p.** = **Harriet, and has issue.**

- **Arthur, Esq., of Placeland, East Grinstead, Sussex.** 1 Arthur Hepburn. 2 Augusta.

- **Caroline Hastie, M.A., Cambs.; Vicar of Great Chishall, Essex.** = **Rev. H. Hastie, M.A., Cambs.; Vicar of Great Chishall, Essex.**

- **Thos. Netherton, a Lt.-Gen., retired, R.A.; b. 1829; educ. Tonbridge School, Kent, and Military Coll., Addiscombe; India 1849 to 1885;**[1]

- **Ellen Haleman, d. and b. of David Edwin Atkinson, of Madras, India.** = **Louisa, b. 1831.**

- **George, Capt. R.A.; b. 1833. See Kinglake, "War in Crimea."**

- **Coningsby, Capt. 13th via, See Foot; b. 1835; d. 1866, s.p.**

- **Eleanor Octavia, b. 1838.** = **J. Thom, Esq., South Park, Bromley, Kent.**

- **Augusta Mary, b. 1840.**

- **Francis Vernon, b. 1844 Rev. Rich. F. Greaves, M.A.** = **Myra, d. of Rev. Rich. F. Greaves, M.A.**

- **Emily, b. 1844.** = **W. Stevenson, of Naval Dublin, Ireland.** Myra, d. and h.

- **Henry, b.1848; Naval and Mil. Club, Piccadilly.**

Next generation:

- **Harry Thos. Colson, b. 1854; d. 1855.**

- **Fredk. Thos. Lane, Manitoba, Canada, b. 1856.**

- **Auberon Geo. Netherton, b. 1860; Cape Mounted Police, Government Educational Dept., South Africa, and has issue.** = **Minnie, dau. of T. Ireland, Esq., of Natal, South Africa.**

- **Arthur J. Netherton, 21st Hussars and Indian Staff Corps; b. 1867.**

- **Annie Harriet Amelia, b. 1864.**

- **Francis Charles William, b. 1870; d. an infant.**

- **James Edward Gainsborough, b. 1871; d. an infant.**

- **Mary Ellen Augusta, b. 1873, and has issue.** = **Fred. Will, son of J. F. Lumsden, Esq.; late B.C.S., of Turner Hall, Ellon, Aberdeensh.**

- **Edith Elinor Alexandra, b. 1875.**

[1] Served in Indian Mutiny Campaign. See Kaye's "Hist. Sepoy War" and despatches.

Appendices.

Index to Appendices.

		PAGE
I.	HEREWARD AS ESQUIRE	101
II.	ATROCIOUS CRUELTY OF WILLIAM I.	102
III.	BELLAMONTE, COUNT OF MELLENT, EARL OF LEICESTER	104
IV.	ROGER LE BIGOD	105
V.	JOHN HARVARD, 1607-38	106
VI.	DERIVATIONS OF HOWARD	108
VII.	HAWARDEN CASTLE	109
VIII.	THE HOWARD CLAIM	109
IX.	KINGSLEY'S "HEREWARD THE WAKE"	111
X.	RICHARD HARWARD, D.D., WARDEN OF ST. CROSS	112
XI.	THE DUCHY OF LANCASTER	113
XII.	HEREWARD OF FRANCTON, CO. WARWICK	116
XIII.	THE COUNTESS LUCIA	116
XIV.	ARMS OF A CONQUERED KNIGHT	118
XV.	SHERIFF HUTTON CASTLE, YORKSHIRE	119
XVI.	ESTATE OF CLEMENT HEREWARD, 1360, BARNINGHAMS	119
	SUPPLEMENTARY NOTES	120

Appendices.

I.

HEREWARD AS ESQUIRE.

SQUIRES, known as armiger, armour-bearer, valet, valeton, or varleton, frequently occur in old writings. All young single men were called "valets," and as the son of a king was named L'enfant, or the Infanta, or Puer, so the words "li vallez" among the French nobility meant "the son of a prince." The term "valet" was almost synonymous with that of "esquire." Thus the "Roman des Loherancs" "La veissez vallez escutenir."[1]

    Esquires were generally young gentlemen who were learning the use of arms. Their education was long and severe: at seven years old the noble children were usually removed from their father's home to the court, or castle, of the future patron, and placed under the care of a governor, who taught them the first articles of religion, respect and reverence to their lords and superiors, and initiated them in the ceremonies of a court. Their office was to carve, to wait at table, and to perform other duties which were not then considered as humiliating. In their leisure hours they learned to dance and play upon the harp, were instructed in hunting, falconry and fishing, and in wrestling, tilting with spears, etc. At fourteen the page became an esquire, and began the course of more laborious exercises. To vault on a horse in heavy armour, to scale walls, and spring over ditches with the same incumbrance, etc., were necessary preliminaries to the reception of knighthood, which was usually conferred at twenty-one years of age. The esquires, whose charge it was to do the honours of the court, acquired those refinements of civility which formed what was called courtesy. Young persons of both sexes assembled in the castle, and the page was encouraged at a very early period to select some lady of the court as the mistress of his heart, to whom he was taught to refer all his sentiments, words and actions. Thus the

---

[1] Note F, p. 126, Mills' "History of the Crusades," fourth edition, 1828, London.

strongest passion of the human heart was so directed as to excel all its witcheries in the cause of virtue. The service of his mistress was the glory and occupation of a knight; her image had taken root in his heart amid the fairy scenes of childhood, and was blended with every recollection of that age of innocence, and her affections, bestowed at once by good-will and gratitude, were held out as the recompense of his well-directed valour (Ellis's Preface to Way's "Translation of French Fables").

In military expeditions the esquire carried the lance, helmet and shield of his knight, and furbished his armour. No service was considered degrading, because the moving principle of a military life is subordination. The squire could not eat at the same table with the cavalier, and if he dared to strike a knight he was punished by the loss of his hand. Some of the duties and qualifications of a squire are described by Chaucer in the "Canterbury Tales."

The training of youth for the profession of arms is referred to in most of the old romances. In the story of the noble and illustrious Helias, Knight of the Swaune, Ydain,[1] the mother of Godfrey de Bouillon and his brothers Baldwin and Eustace, thus educated her sons:

"When in their adolescence they were somewhat comen to the age of strengthe, they began to practyse them in shooting with their bows and arbelstre; to play with the swerde and buckeler, to run, to just, to play with a pollaxe, and to wrastle"; and in due time, as the chronicle relates, they were each sent to the Emperor of Almayne[2] to be knighted.

It is to be deplored that, with few exceptions, a mere cramming with theory is substituted for the efficient education in arms and manly sports herein described in the case of modern candidates for military distinction.

II.

ATROCIOUS CRUELTY OF WILLIAM I.

THE most strongly-marked characteristic of William was the violent and cruel spirit, which seemed inseparable from his rule, in every action. In all the histories of his career no single act of mercy or gentle conduct is recorded. Of illegitimate birth—his mother was of low social position, and his father generally known as Robert the Devil—he came into the world under great disadvantages of blood and breeding, which he took little pains to improve. His constant quarrels with his own sons, his cruelties to the English peasantry, and his miserable death, place him almost beyond the reach of human sympathies.

When his own town of Alençon rebelled, hanging out skins in allusion to his maternal origin, and shouting, "La pel al parmentier"—"Hides for the clothier!"—he avenged himself by taking the town by assault and cutting off the hands and feet of two-and-thirty of the garrison, a barbarism which afterwards became quite ordinary in his subsequent rule of Saxon England. The violence of temper and ferocity of his nature did not spare his own wife,

---

[1] Ida.   [2] Germany.

Appendices.

Matilda, the grand-daughter of a king of France, from the basest insult and brutal cruelty. On one occasion he forced his way into her chamber, dragged her by the hair, and, dashing her upon the floor, spurned and trampled upon her. On another occasion he intercepted her on her way home from church at Bruges, and brutally beat her and wounded her with his spurs.[1]

Who but a butcher would have feasted and slept amidst the piles of the dead and groans of the dying in the slaughter-house of the entrenchment at Senlac, the holy lake of blood of the Saxon martyrs who fell in the battle for England, home, and duty? On his deathbed he acknowledged himself to be the murderer of many thousands, old and young. How many men had he not caused to be brutally maimed and blinded, not for rebellion, theft or violence, but for some trifling offence connected with the sumptuary or forest laws he so unjustly enacted!

In no other country has such a wholesale system of rapine, spoliation and severity been recorded. The divine right of kings is to execute justice with mercy. "Parce regibus" is a maxim to be applied to sovereigns who commit pardonable errors. Unless history is to become a colourless jumble or partial record, as such historians as Freeman will make it, it cannot spare the memory of so vile a man as William I. In all time to come the bloodstain will rest upon him, and in every English home the agonized voices of the poor Saxon peasantry, murdered, maimed and robbed by his orders, will drown any appeal he can make for the merciful verdict of posterity.

With much regret is this painful statement placed on record in defence of the harsh but not unjust opinions expressed in the body of this work when referring to William's acts and character. In conclusion, a modernized Anglo-Saxon poem from the "Chronicle," A.D. 1087, will give an insight to contemporary opinion of the Conqueror:

> "Gold he took by might,
> And of great unright,
> From his folk with evil deed
> For sou little need.
> He was on greediness befallen,
> And getsomeness he loved withal.
> He set a mickle deer frith,
> And he laid laws therewith,
> That whoso slew hart or hind
> Him should man then blinden.
> He forbade to slay the harts,
> And so eke the boars.
> And so well he loved the high deer,
> As if he their father were.
> Eke he set by the hares,
> That they might freely fare.
> His rich men mourned it,
> And the poor man wailed it.

See "The Conqueror and his Companions," by J. R. Planché, Somerset Herald. William of Malmesbury records that Matilda was beaten to death with a horse's bridle.

But he was so firmly wrought
That he wrecked of all nought.
And they must all withal
The King's will follow,
If they wished to live
Or their lands have,
Or their goods eke,
Or his peace to seek.
Woe is me
That any man so proud should be,
Thus himself up to raise,
And over all men to boast.
May God Almighty show his soul mild-heartedness,
And do him for his sins forgiveness![1]

III.

BELLAMONTE, COUNT OF MELLENT, EARL OF LEICESTER.

WHEN William the Norman prepared to invade England, he called to his aid, not only his subjects of Normandy, but men from Maine and Anjou, from Poictou and Brittany, from the country of the French King, and from Flanders, from Aquitaine, and from Burgundy, from Piedmont beyond the Alps, and from the German countries beyond the Rhine. The soldier-robbers, who called murder "war" and plunder "ransom," flocked from all parts of Europe to his standard. Some demanded pay in money, others a passage across the Channel and the booty they might take; some of the chiefs demanded territory in England, while others simply bargained for a rich English wife. William sold a bishopric in England for a ship and twenty men-at-arms. The Pope gave him a licence to invade England, and sent a bull, a consecrated banner, and a ring of great price containing one of the hairs of St. Peter. The armament is said to have consisted of 3,000 vessels, of which 500 or 600 were of good size.

Robert Beaumont, or Bellamonte, Count de Mellent in right of his wife, was a worthy descendant of the pirate-chiefs who overran France and Neustria. A free-lance, ever ready to sell himself and his men-at-arms to the highest bidder, he possessed a certain amount of tact, avoiding force when he could gain his ends by fraud. Cotemporary writers speak respectfully of his power of acquiring wealth together with towns and castles, villages and farms, woods and waters. There is much irony in the remark that he obtained all this plunder "by the exercise of his talents." It is also stated that he held domains in England, Normandy and France, and that he was able at will to promote concord, or set the kings at variance and provoke them to war. Such men were the curse of the Mediæval Period, equally unscrupulous in their methods of acquiring wealth, and dead to all the claims of humanity.

[1] This poem is extracted from "Anglo-Saxon Britain," by Grant Allen; published by the Society for Promoting Christian Knowledge.

He pretended to a descent from the Kings of Denmark, and actually sat as a Peer of France in 1082 in a provincial Parliament held at Poissy. Owing fealty to France and England, he transferred his allegiance as self-interest dictated, but attached himself chiefly to England. He was made Earl of Leicester, and nearly all the estates of Hereward and those of his father, Leofric, Earl of Mercia, as well as those of Alfgar, his brother, and Edwin and Morkar, his nephews, were assigned to Count Mellent *in capite.* Some portion was given as a dower to the Countess Lucia, daughter of Alfgar. Dying in 1118, he was succeeded by his second son, Robert Bossu (hunchback), in the English estates and earldom.

His domestic relations were of a nature that precluded his wives living with him. His first wife, Godechilde de Couches, obtained a divorce, and married Baldwin, King of Jerusalem. His second wife, Isabella, daughter of Hugh, Comte de Vermandois, by whom he had issue, left him also, and eloped with William Warren, Earl of Surrey, and ancestor of the Dukes of Norfolk. His family, which lasted four generations, was only remarkable for Simon de Montfort, who married his grand-daughter, Amicia, and in default of heirs male succeeded to the family honours and estates. He united a royal liberality of mind with truly patriotic courage, and was killed at the battle of Evesham, when the Hereward, Mercian and Mellent Estates were conferred upon Edmund, second son of Henry III., and afterwards swelled the coffers of the Duchy of Lancaster.

The Dukes of Hamilton claim descent from Count Mellent, or Meulan (the Mill), alleging that his name was Hambledon, whence Hamilton. It was, however, Bellamonte. The second Earl of Leicester was the son of Count Mellent, called Robert Bossu; the third Earl, Robert Blanchmains; and the fourth Earl, Fitz-Parnell. Leaving no heirs male, Simon de Montfort, grandson of Adeline, daughter of Robert, second Earl of Mellent, who married Hugh, fourth Sire de Montfort-sur-Rislein, 1206, having married his cousin Amicia, sister and co-heir of Fitz-Parnell, Earl of Leicester, succeeded to his title and estates.

IV.

ROGER LE BIGOD.

ROGER LE BIGOD, like most of the mushroom "lords" who established themselves in England at the Conquest, was of humble origin. His father, Robert, was a servant of William I. After the battle at Senlac he received a large share of plunder, six manors in Essex, and 118 in Suffolk.

His father was seneschal, or butler, to William, and Roger succeeded him, being also appointed Privy Councillor and treasurer to the two Williams. He was also seneschal to Henry I. His two sons, William and Hugh, succeeded him in the office.

Roger survived the Conquest forty-three years. He built and fortified the castle of Norwich. The usual Norman cruelties being practised upon the people, they fled the country, and the whole of the Norwich district was laid waste. By Henry I. he had Framlingham, in Suffolk, given to him. He

founded the Abbey of Thetford, and was buried there. He married Adeliza, daughter and co-heir of Hugh de Grentmesnil, by whom he had seven children :
1. William, styled Dapifer regis Anglorum.
2. Hugh le Bigod, first Earl of Norfolk.
3. Richard.
4. Geoffrey.
5. John.
6. Maud, wife of William de Albini Pincerna.
7. Gunnora, married, first, Robert of Essex ; second, Hamo di Clare.

William perished in the *White Ship* with the heir to the throne, and Hugh, created Earl of Norfolk, married Maud, daughter and co-heiress of the Earl of Pembroke, Marshal of England, which dignity has ever since been borne by Earls and Dukes of Norfolk.

The vulgar name Bigod, with prefix "le," indicates the low origin of the Earls of Norfolk. It is sometimes spelt "Bihot," " Bigot," " Vegot," " Wihot," but is clearly a nickname given to them from their constantly using the expression. If the name had been derived from land the prefix would have been " de," not " le." A somewhat far-fetched derivation suggests that Vigot may come from Visigoth, a tribe of Scythians.

The Earls Bigot of Norfolk only held their lands for five generations, during which period Theodore de Hereward and his son William held lands of them. The family then became extinct. In 4 Henry IV. we find Mowbray, Lord and Duke of Norfolk, and he was succeeded by one De Wygenhale, who took the name of Howard.

For this notice we are largely indebted to Planché, Somerset Herald.

V.

JOHN HARVARD,[1] 1607-38.

FOUNDER OF HARVARD UNIVERSITY, MASSACHUSETTS, U.S.A.

ROBERT, the father of John Harvard, lived in the parish of St. Saviour, Southwark, for many years. His business was probably that of a butcher or meat salesman.[2] He died in the first plague, 1625, when six of his family were carried off, the only survivors being his wife and two sons, John and Thomas.

The Harvards of Southwark were descended from an offshoot of the Herwards of Norfolk and Warwickshire, as we find John Herward, gent., was resident in the parish of St. Mary Magdalene, Southwark, and died in 1487.[3] A colony of Danes had settled in St. Mary Overies, the old name of St. Saviour's, and the name Herward in Saxon became Harvard[4] in Danish.

[1] Etymology, *Heorn* (Anglo-Saxon or Danish), a sword ; *vard*, a guard : hence Heornvard, or Hereward, was the sword-guardian (Miss Charlotte Yonge, "Christian Names," p. 356).
[2] Exact site of house uncertain. Probably in one of a row of shops opposite Boar's Head Court.
[3] Will in Prerogative Court of Canterbury, 1487.
[4] Except in this instance, the name had not been so spelt since the tenth century.

Appendices.

The will of William Harward, gent., of "Blakfreres," dated 1525 (F. 3, Porch), is also at Canterbury. In 1609 Thomas Harward, of the Merchant Taylors' Company, subscribed 10s. to the Bachelors' Company of Virginia, the profits to be given in charity.

It seems therefore natural that Robert Harvard should have gone back to Warwickshire to find a wife. In Shakespeare's town he married Katherine, daughter of Thomas and Margaret Rogers. Mr. Rogers[1] was an Alderman of Stratford-on-Avon. His house there, still existing as "Ye ancient house," is a fair specimen of the architecture of the period. On the front, under a broad oriel window, is inscribed "TR 1596 AR."

The register of Robert Harvard's marriage is: "1605 Apriell 8 Robertus Harwod to Katherine Rogers." An illiterate parson would try to spell Harward phonetically. The incident proves that "v" was peculiar to the Danish parish. In Southwark vestry records the name was often mis-spelt, but in five out of seven instances noted with a "v."[2]

On the death of Robert, his widow married secondly John Ellison, or Elleton, who died June, 1626. She then married Richard Yearwood, or Yerwood, Esq., M.P. for Southwark, and survived him. She made a will in 1635 in favour of his two sons, John and Thomas, and died in 1637.

The Queen's Head Inn was left to John,[3] but it passed from his hands in 1637, when he married and went to America. Richard Yearwood, stepfather to John, was first cousin to Sir G. Yardley, or Yeardley, appointed Governor of Virginia March 14, 1626, and this connection may have had an influence on John's career. Richard Yearwood was M.P. for Southwark 1614, 1621-22, 1624-26, 1628. He left a good fortune to his descendants, who are scattered over the United States of America.

John Harvard was baptized in St. Saviour's, November 29, 1607, entered Emanuel College, Cambridge, December 19, 1627, graduated B.A. in 1631, and M.A. in 1635. As a Churchman he held liberal views, and may not have agreed with Archbishop Laud. He visited America in 1630; in 1637 his mother died; he married Ann, daughter of Rev. John Sadler, a Sussex clergyman, and, having disposed of his estate, he sailed for New England. In the same year he was made a freeman of the colony of Massachusetts, and in 1638 a member of the Committee for Legislation. He died of consumption September 14, 1638. He was a godly gentleman and a lover of learning.

The Harvard University, near Boston, Massachusetts, U.S.A., was founded by him with a moiety of his fortune and his library of books. He resided some time at Charleston, and is said to have preached there.

His last resting-place was in the graveyard, Charleston, where a monument has been erected. At Harvard he is commemorated by an ideal bronze statue, inscribed on the plinth, "John Harvard, Founder." In the chapel of Emanuel College, Cambridge, eight windows are dedicated to theologians. In the third window on the north side is John Harvard, with Lawrence Chader-

---

[1] His will was proved at Worcester, April, 1611. The register of his marriage at Stratford, Thos. Rogers to Marg^t. Pace, is dated January 31, 1562.
[2] Hayward, Harver, Harwood, Harvye, Harverd, Harvey and Harvie.
[3] The Harvard wills are of course extant, and have been copied by Mr. Waters, of Massachusetts. The signatures of two sons are on a deed in St. Katherine's Hospital.—*Athenæum*, December 10, 1887.

ton, first Master of Emanuel, as his companion. In John Harvard's hand is a scroll with "Populus qui creabitur laudabit Dominum."

VI.

DERIVATIONS OF HOWARD.

VERSTEGEN, in his "Restitution of Decayed Intelligence," London, 1634, p. 320, has the following derivation of Howard :

"Holdward. This ancient and honorable name of office hath received the injury of time, which hath worn it out of use and memory.

"The *l* and *d* being for easiness of sound omitted in the pronunciation, as in sundry other words the like is seen, it became of Holdward, which signifieth the governor, or keeper, of a castle, fort, or holde of warre, to be Howard.

"Which name of office albeit we have long since lost, yet retaineth our realm to the high honor and illustrious ornament thereof, the great and right noble family unto whom it is now the bearing of such a warlike, honorable office and charge."

The above derivation may be correct, and the French "Huard" may have been derived from Holdward, contracted Howard ; or "Huard" may come from Hugihard, "firm in mind," from Scan. "hargr."

Then again, we have the derivation from how, "a hill" (Saxon), and ward, "a guard," so care of, or guardianship of, a castle.

Mr. Walter Rye, in his "History of Norfolk," 1887, deduces the name, which was spelt "Haward" by Sir W. Wygenhale, the judge who first took the name of Howard, from Hayward, or Heyward, a rural officer subordinate to the reeve, first appointed by the Normans.

Howardus is the name recorded in Domesday, and with such authority we may be content, though the etymological derivation of the name may still afford occupation to the curious.

Howardus would become Houard in Normandy.

This note would not be complete without a quotation from the work (1893) of the late Dean of Ripon, Dr. Isaac Taylor, a most learned etymologist.

"The surnames Hayward and Howard are corruptions of Hogwarden, an officer elected annually to see that the swine in the common forest pastures or dens were duly provided with rings and were prevented from straying. The Howard family first come into notice in the Weald, where their name would lead us to expect to find them. So the family name of Woodward is 'veard,' the wood warden whose duties were analogous to those of the Howard. There are many evidences of the importance attached to swine in Anglo-Saxon times. Flitch is etymologically the same word as 'fleisch,' or 'flesh,' showing that the flesh of swine was pre-eminently 'the flesh' to which our ancestors were accustomed. Sir Walter Scott has pointed out in 'Ivanhoe' that while beef, veal, mutton, are Norman terms, bacon is Saxon."

Who shall be wise when learned men cannot agree ? Dugdale's advice to the Earl Marshal, under whom he served as Garter King at arms, ought to have been followed in respect to the family pedigree of the distinguished House of Howard.

VII.

HAWARDEN CASTLE, FLINTSHIRE.

IN Domesday Book this ancient castle is called Hedoine. It was a defensive post on the marches of Wales of much importance, in charge of the Earls of Chester and Mercia. At the Conquest it was in possession of Edwin, the last Earl of Mercia, son of Alfgar, and nephew of Hereward, and "Hedoine" Castle, as recorded in Domesday, was probably "Edwin's" Castle. It was built as a defence against the Britons of Wales, but Alfgar appears to have established friendly relations with the Welsh through Gruffydd, or Griffith, King of North Wales, who married Alfgar's daughter. Hedoine was a chief manor of the Hundred of Atiscross. At Domesday it was a lordship with a church, two carucæ of arable land, of which half a one belonged to the church, one half-acre meadow, and wood two leagues in length, and half a league broad. The whole value forty shillings. Upon it were four villeyns, six boors, four slaves.

William gave the castle to Hugh Lupus, who was made Earl of Chester, but it was for some time held by the Barons of Mont alto, Montalt, or Mold, as Stewards of the Earl. The castle and church were probably built by Leofric III., Earl of Chester and Mercia, who endowed numerous churches and monasteries in Mercia. The history of the castle is yet to be written. It was believed to possess one of the finest dungeons in England, vying with Pontefract Castle.

VIII.

THE HOWARD CLAIM.

IN the "Popular History of Norfolk," 1887,[1] Howard, Duke of Norfolk, Premier Peer and Earl Marshal of England, is thus noticed : "This family descends from Sir W. Howard, who was on the Bench in 1293, whose real pedigree is very obscure and doubtful, and who invariably spelt his name Haward. There is great reason to believe that Haward is simply Heyward, defined by Halliwell as the person who guarded the farmyard by night. His pedigree was concocted very carelessly, and can deceive no one. It traces the Howards to Auber, Earl of Passy, in Normandy, whose grandson, Roger Fitz Valerine, "is said to have owned the castle of Howarden, or Howard's den. Alliances with the Bigods, the St. Meres, the Bardolphs, the Brus, and the Trusbuts, are liberally provided to bring in nice-looking quarterings, while an alternative descent from Hereward is also put forward. Unluckily the matches are absent from the very well known pedigrees of the families in question, and as to the Bigod match, Maud Bigod was living in 1245, while her alleged great-great-great-great grandson, the judge, was a judge in 1293 ! The whole of this fiction has now been abandoned by the family."

[1] By Walter Rye, editor of the "Norfolk Antiquarian Miscellany," published by Elliot Stock, Paternoster Row.

Herewardi Arbor Gentis.

In the face of such an indictment, little credit can be given to any future claim of family the Howards may advance.

Two different statements are now extant in Burke's "Peerages" of 1862 and 1867.

In 1862 Dugdale is quoted thus: "There are those, perhaps, who will expect that I should ascend much higher in *manifesting the greatness* of this honourable and large-spreading family of Howard, in regard I do not make any mention thereof above the time of Edward I., some supposing that their common ancestor in the Saxon time took his original appellation from an eminent office or command[1]; others afterwards from the name of a place.[2] And some have not stuck to derive him from the famous Hereward, the chief conductor of those forces which so stoutly defended the Isle of Ely for a time against William the Conqueror and his army; but to this last I cannot well assent, by reason that Ingulph, then Abbot of Croyland, who was his contemporary, affirms that Hereward left no other issue than heir female, named Turfrida, wife to Hugh de Evermue, Lord of Deping, co. Lincoln.[3] I shall therefore, after much fruitless search to satisfy myself, as well as others, on this point, begin with William Howard,[4] a learned and reverend judge of the Court of Common Pleas for a great part of the reign of Edward I."

Now, Sir W. Dugdale was Garter King at Arms under Henry Howard, sixth Duke of Norfolk, and would naturally have done all in his power in favour of the genealogy of his chief, and his exhaustive opinion given above seems to close the pedigree at Sir W. Howard, notwithstanding the evidence of Domesday and the "Historia Ecclesiæ Eliensis."

In 1867 that unfortunate desire of still further "manifesting his greatness" decided the "Premier Duke immediately after the princes of the blood royal" to put aside erasers, penknives, acids, and such like vulgar weapons of forgery, and boldly to declare that Howard and Hereward were one and indivisible! The following narration was concocted and published about 1867: "Norfolk, Duke of. — Is the chief of the family of Howard, a family undoubtedly[5] of Saxon origin. Recent enquiries enable us to trace the ancestors of the Howards to a period much more remote than Sir Wm. Dugdale thought possible, and to establish the pedigree by undoubted evidence.[6] Ingulph and Matthew Paris concur in stating that Howard, or Hereward,[7] was living in the reign of King Edgar, 957-973, and that his son Leofric was the father of Hereward, who was banished by the Conqueror.[8] The very ancient book of the Church of Ely, "Historia Ecclesia Eliensis," entirely confirms the statement. It appears that Hereward was subsequently allowed to return, and it

[1] "How" in Saxon a hill or mound, "ward," care; so care of a castle.
[2] Harwardine, written "Hedoine" in Domesday.—ED.
[3] The bequest of land by Hereward's grandson, noted in "Liber Ecclesiæ Eliensis," refutes Ingulph.
[4] As a matter of fact, the judge's name was Sir William de Wygenhal, and he brought the Howards reputation and wealth, and was the first of the family to emerge from obscurity.
[5] One would think that the claim of kin to Auber, Earl of Passy, in Normandy, had never been made. Beware, reader, of alleged "certainties" from an unreliable source.
[6] For "undoubted" read "improbable."
[7] It is assumed, in the face of the strongest evidence to the contrary, that the names Hereward and Howard are identical.
[8] The actual truth is that he was banished by Edward the Confessor, and restored by William. Leofric's father was Leofwine.

is certain[1] that his family retained Wigenhall and other portions of their inheritance in Norfolk. Hereward's grandson, Hereward, or Howard, and his wife Wilburga, in the reign of Henry II. granted a carucate of land at Torrington,[2] in Norfolk, to the Church of Len (Lynn), and directed that prayers should be said for the souls of Hereward, his father, and of Hereward the banished, or the exile, his grandfather. Robert Howard, the son of Hereward, was seised of Wigenhall and other estates in Norfolk, and was the father of John Hereward, or Howard, of Wigenhall, who, by Lucy Germond, his wife, was the father of Sir Wm. Howard, the judge."

It will be observed the point in this story is whether Hereward and Howard are identical. Until that can be shown by evidence we cannot in reason accept it as a statement of fact.

The spelling of ancient names is no doubt found to vary, and we know that the Heralds' College attaches little importance to differences in spelling, but the line must be drawn somewhere, and the only reasonable and satisfactory test is that of etymological inference.[3] Every authority is opposed to the Duke of Norfolk's contention, and the evidence of *mala fides*[4] in establishing the fictitious Howard pedigrees is so strong that no Court of Honour would suffer this claim to pass without the most careful analysis and the clearest proof.

IX.

KINGSLEY'S "HEREWARD THE WAKE."

A REVIEWER[5] takes the Rev. C. Kingsley severely, but justly, to task for his mad escapade as Professor of English History in twisting the hero of these pages, the renowned Hereward, into a peg on which to hang a Northampton family named Wake or Jones. A silly archbishop of their name misspent his time in weaving the fiction, and a still more foolish prebendary turns a somersault over the professorial chair, and produces his abortive "Hereward the Wake; the last of the English!"

Our reviewer acknowledges that Kingsley could once be a novelist, a historian never; because "he cannot appreciate or understand history; he cannot discern truth from falsehood." He alleges the real culprit to be not Mr. Kingsley, "but those who put a man in a historical chair who lacks

---

[1] No one of the name of Hereward ever possessed Wigenhall. It was bought probably by Sir W. Howard, who was known as Sir William de Wygenhall.

[2] The Herewards were for many years connected with Terrington, or Taunton, as it is called. Sir John Hereward, Archdeacon of Terrington, was one of the commissioners appointed by Edward II. to appear before the council at Avignon, held by the Pope (1334), to decide upon Edward III.'s claim to the throne of France, through his mother, Isabella of Valois, daughter of Philip, King of France, by default direct of heirs male. The claim failed owing to the Salique law, and the result was invasion, the battles of Crecy and Poictiers, and the humiliation of France.

[3] Travesties of names, especially those of Norman origin, are to be met with in fact and fiction, and it requires some ingenuity to reconcile them to their origin. Thus, De Nouailles has become Nowell; De Bayeux, Debbyhouse; Paridelles, Priddles; De Couci, Dicksee; and so with many other distinguished historical names.

[4] See also note 1, p. 5, Chapter iii.

[5] *Saturday Review*, May 19, 1866.

every qualification of a historian." He then instances the title of the book in disproof of the Professor's claim to accuracy, especially as to "the Wake."

As Mr. Kingsley poses as a historian in this book, and goes out of his way to challenge criticism, the reviewer judges him on his own ground. He alludes to the "daring falsifications of history" in "Hypatia," and describes the fall from "Hypatia" to "Hereward" as "a fall which words can hardly express."

Referring to Hereward and history, the reviewer some years ago had occasion to review a brochure by Mr. Trollope, a Lincolnshire antiquary, who has been accepted by Mr. Kingsley as a shining light, for "Among the blind the one-eyed man is king." He then enters upon a discussion as to the alleged parentage of Hereward and his marriages, which I omit. The critic, however, disputes Hereward's descent from the Earl of Mercia, but allows that his father's name was Leofric.

The inaccuracy of Mr. Kingsley's facts and deductions is severely commented upon. "Mr. Kingsley's boast throughout is that he sticks close to the facts. For 'facts' we venture to read 'fictions.'" Step by step we are shown how Mr. Kingsley, shutting both eyes, has allowed himself to be misled by fictitious romances, until at last he has taken as historical facts the statements of a legendary story, or, as in the case of the alleged encounter in his book between Edgar Atheling and Hereward, he indulges in pure imagination, and calls it history! He adds: "Mr. Kingsley has thrown away his great opportunity" (of writing a good romance on an excellent theme), "and has written instead a mere roaring, rollicking, boisterous story."

The ludicrous Wake episode is thus touched upon: "One crowning absurdity more, and we have done with our Professor. The family of Wake claim descent from Hereward, whether with any truth or not we do not know. The name of 'le Wake' is given to Hereward for the first time by 'John of Peterborough,' an author of uncertain date—perhaps as late as the fifteenth century. There is nothing like it in the earlier legends, nothing in the 'De Gestis,' nothing in 'Ingulf,' nothing in 'Gaimar,' nothing in the 'History of Ely.' But Mr. Kingsley calls Hereward 'the Wake' throughout,[1] and puts the words into his own mouth."

In conclusion the reviewer adds: "His friends will certainly desire to keep his lectures in manuscript, while his enemies will wish for nothing better than to see them in print."

X.

RICHARD HARWARD, D.D.

The Rev. R. Harward, D.D., Warden of St. Cross.—The Rev. Richard Harward, D.D., was appointed Warden of St. Cross by Cardinal Beaufort, then Bishop of Winchester,[2] about 1445, to aid in the development of the new endowment of the almshouses for the brethren of "noble poverty,"

[1] For which he was most liberally remunerated.
[2] The Bishop, no doubt, desired his hospital at St. Cross to vie with that of Archbishop Abbot at Guildford, and to be on a larger scale, but it has been terribly mismanaged, whilst the Abbot Hospital is flourishing.

Appendices.

consisting of thirty-five brothers, three sisters, and two priests, in addition to the ancient trusts created in the time of Henry I., three hundred years earlier. In 1557 the Beaufort trust had ceased to exist. The trustees pulled down their own buildings, and used the Beaufort quadrangle for their own purposes—now a brewery! The lands seem to have been disposed of, and the present endowment yields only £1,800 a year, but when the leases fall in will be worth £8,000 annually.

One of the most remarkable English prelates in our Church history was also a Warden of St. Cross, the Rev. Henry Compton, D.D., sometime Canon of Christ Church, Bishop of Oxford, and Dean of the Chapel Royal. He earnestly endeavoured to reconcile Dissenters to the Church, and was persecuted by James II. for his orthodox Protestantism, being dismissed from the deanery and suspended from his bishopric.

His first act in the Revolution was to escort the Princess Anne, to whom he had been appointed guardian by Charles II., to Nottingham, in "a buff coat and jack boots, with pistols in his holsters and a sword by his side." He afterwards crowned William and Mary.

The Hospital of St. Cross was first established by Bishop Henry de Blois, who placed it in the care of the Knights of St. John of Jerusalem, called the Hospitallers, as their duty was to relieve distress. Their connection with St. Cross is still shown in the dress of the brethren, who wear a black cloak with the white cross of the order upon the left breast.

The endowments have been tampered with, but the hospitality of St. Cross is still maintained, bread and ale being offered to all comers who require such aid.

XI.

THE DUCHY OF LANCASTER.

THE Duchy of Lancaster was chiefly formed by the spoliation of the family and descendants of the Earls of Mercia.

The titles borne by the Earls of Mercia, as recorded at Croyland Abbey and Coventry, were Earl of Leicester, Earl of Lincoln, Earl of Chester, until Leofric III. became Earl of Mercia, his son Alfgar being Earl of East Anglia in his father's lifetime, and subsequently Earl of Mercia. Alfgar's sons, Edwin, Earl of Mercia, and Morcar, were also Earls of Warwick and Northumberland.

The rebellion of Edwin and Morcar, after having taken an oath of allegiance to William, may have justified the temporary alienation of their estates, but it will be seen from evidence in the reports of the Deputy-Keeper of the Public Records that the estates which in the first instance devolved upon the Countess Lucia, sister of Edwin and Morcar, and which should have descended to the representatives of her uncle Hereward, were entirely absorbed into the Duchy of Lancaster. Hereward's lands had been made over *in capite* to the Earl of Mellent, whose son and grandson received the Mercian title of Earl of Leicester, which by right should have gone with his estates to Hereward.

Simon de Montfort, Earl of Leicester, married the sole heiress of the

Earl of Mellent, and on her death Henry III.'s sister, Eleanor. He endeavoured to reform the abuses of the kingdom, again overrun by needy adventurers from Poitou and Provence, by establishing the first Parliament with a House of Lords and a House of Commons. In the civil war which ensued Simon de Montfort, one of England's truest patriots, was slain with his son at the battle of Evesham, 1265. His estates were confiscated and conferred upon Edmund, second son of Henry III., and thus the estates of the Earl of Mercia, as well as those of Hereward, formed the foundation of the Duchy of Lancaster.

Gilbert of Ghent became Earl of Lincoln by right of his wife, Rohais de Romara, a lineal descendant of the Countess Lucy, daughter of Alfgar, Earl of Mercia. This Gilbert took the surname of Lucy, Lacy, or Lacie, from his wife Lucia. He was one of the wealthiest peers in England. Originally the representative of the Flemish nation, he had been careful of their commercial rights in the woollen trade, their staple manufacture. He acquired vast estates in fourteen counties, with castles, mills, and houses (see Domesday). Appointed by William I. to the custody of Lincoln Castle, he avoided collision with Hereward in the Camp of Refuge, and would no doubt have befriended him actively, if he had not had so much to lose, for he was his godfather.

Thomas, the eldest son of the above Edmund, second son of Henry III., married Alice, daughter and heiress of Henry Lacy de Ghent, grandson of Gilbert, Earl of Lincoln, and his father having already secured the estates of the Mercian family, which had been confiscated to the Earl of Mellent, the remainder, which had formed the dower of the Countess Lucy, now fell into the hands of the Plantagenet Earl of Lancaster, and, by right of his wife, Earl of Lincoln, and the Herewards as the male descendants of Leofric III. of Mercia were disinherited.

Thomas, beheaded for alleged treason in the 15th year of Edward II. of Carnarvon, was succeeded in the earldom of Lancaster by his brother Henry, whose son Henry, created Duke of Lancaster, left two daughters and coheiresses, Maud and Blanche, the latter of whom married John, born at Ghent, and called John of Gaunt, or Ghent, third son of Edward III.

In the Appendix to the Thirty-fifth Report of the Deputy-Keeper of the Public Records, we learn how the princely appanage of the Crown of England, called the Duchy of Lancaster, was first formed.

In the explanatory remarks to the Calendar of Ancient Charters or Grants, it is stated that the estates "to which these grants have reference subsequently vested in the Earls and Dukes of Lancaster by alliances with the inheritors and representatives of those families who owned them, including the Earl of Chester (Mellent, and afterwards Simon de Montfort), de Lacy (Earl of Lincoln, whose ancestor married Lucia, daughter of Earl Alfgar, and niece of Hereward), De Bohun, Chaworth, and De Quince." The duchy is practically composed of the estates of the two first families.

The statement that the estates held by Count Mellent, Earl of Chester, vested in the Earls and Dukes of Lancaster by marriage, is absolutely incorrect, and almost unfounded. The estates which in Domesday belonged *in capite* to Hereward before the Conquest were confiscated by William, not by Edward the Confessor, and the fee conferred upon Count Mellent, Hereward being permitted to retain some of the lands as under-tenant. In the fourth generation afterwards the Mellent estates had fallen to Simon de Montfort, who was accused of treason, and his estates forfeited. De Montfort's treason consisted in his establishing Parliaments in which the people were properly represented.

In 1266,[1] when Robert de Ferrers, Earl of Derby, was also plundered, the honour of Leicester, and with it the title of Earl of Leicester, was taken from Simon de Montfort, and conferred upon Edmund, second son of Henry III. In the same year, in the same way—by simple plunder—Edmund acquired Kenilworth Castle and the castle of Builth.

In 1267[2] the three castles, Grosmont, Skenfreth, and Whitnearth, were added to the plunder, together with the honour of Lancaster (giving the title of Earl of Lancaster), Newcastle-under-Lyme, the honour of Pickering, manors of Scalby, Godmanchester, and Huntingdon. The Earl of Huntingdon was outlawed during these proceedings, and for many a long year afterwards was immortalized as "Robin Hood" in the merry Sherwood Forest. The rapacious Edmund, who was a nephew of Simon de Montfort by his marriage with Eleanor, sister of Henry III., also obtained in 1269 the stewardship of England, formerly held by Simon de Montfort, as well as a grant of all De Montfort possessed. In 1271 another charter granted him ten other manors of Simon de Montfort's. Thus, it is clear that the Duchy of Lancaster became possessed of these properties by wholesale spoliation and the right of the strongest, and not, as claimed by the officials, by descent or purchase.

The grandson of Henry III. certainly married the heiress of the Earl of Lincoln (De Lacy), descended from Gilbert of Ghent, Hereward's godfather, but the greater portion of the estates of the Duchy of Lancaster were derived from the forfeiture and confiscations of Simon de Montfort, Earl of Leicester, who succeeded to the estates of the Earls of Mercia, misappropriated by the ancestor of his father-in-law, the Earl of Mellent. To provide for this and similar cases the law invented an aphorism, "The King can do no wrong." "What, never? Hardly ever."

It may be convenient to insert for reference, as well as for the confusion of J. R. Planché, Somerset Herald, and others, who deny the existence and marriages of the Countess Lucy, a copy of the endorsement of Charters in the Record Office, referred to in the Appendix to the Thirty-fifth Report of the Deputy-Keeper of Public Records:

"69 S.D. (1135-1154).—Grant in fee by Wm. Roumara, made for the soul of his mother Lucia, daughter of Algar, Earl of Chester, to Robert, nephew or grandson (*nepoti*) of the Countess of the land of Ivo and Colsuenus, uncles of the said Robert, held of the said William's mother (Lucia). Witnesses eleven.

"69*a* S.D. (1152-1188). — Confirmation of above grant by Wm. de Roumara, grandson of the donor, in favour of Robert, son of Robert, nephew of the Countess. Witnesses and seal."

[1] See Appendix to Thirty-first Report of Deputy-Keeper of Records, No. I., Duchy of Lancaster.
[2] *Ibid.*, No. O.

The seal of Rohais, daughter of the above William Roumara, inscribed "Sigill. Hais Vxoris Gilleber E. Gant," is in the British Museum, No. 164 in the catalogue. She became Countess of Lincoln in her own right on the death of her father, and conferred the title of Earl upon her husband Gilbert, Earl of Ghent, great-grandson of Hereward's godfather.

XII.

HEREWARD OF FRANKTON, CO. WARWICK.

FRANKTON (Domesday, Francheton), co. Warwick. Some property and the advowson of the living of Frankton came to Jno. Hereward in the beginning of Hen. VI. by Kath., dau. and heir of Thos. Palmer, descended from Will. le Palmere, 20 Ed. III. (1347 A.D.), who with Hen. de Hinton held half a knight's fee (1 cart., Warwick Com.). The advowson in 4 Ed. II. (1311 A.D.) was aliened to John le Palmere, of Frankton, and his heirs, with one messu., 2 yards land, 3 acres meadow, and 3s. 1d. rent, by Ralph de Okeover, who had it from Rog. de Elinhale, who had it from Will. de Frankton, who held from the Earl of Warwick one knight's fee, "de veteri feoffmenti."

"John Hereward et uxor ejus filia et hæres T. Palmer de Frankton" instituted incumbents.—Pracy, 1427, Coventie, 1451.

PATRONI ECCLESIÆ FRANKTON.

Rob. de Hokeover	- 1305	A.D.
John le Palmere	- 1338	,,
Will. le Palmere	- 1346	,,
Jno. le Palmere	- 1350	,,
D. Episcopus	- 1372	,,
Thos. Palmer	- 1408	,,
Jno. Hereward et uxor ejus	- 1427	,,

Reynburn Balgis vice Ric. Duke, who held it from the beginning of Hen. VIII.

The church was first endowed by Leofrike, Earl of Mercia.

The present collateral representative of the le Palmeres of Frankton should be found in the family of the Rev. Charles Palmer, of Ladbroke, co. Warwick, married, 23 Jan., 1823, Lady Charlotte, god-daughter of King Geo. IV. and daughter of Heneage Finch, 4th Earl of Aylesford, of Packington Hall, Coventry, Warwick.—Extract chiefly from Dugdale.

XIII.

THE COUNTESS LUCIA.

LUCIA, sister of the Earls Edwin and Morcar, and daughter of Alfgar III., Earl of Mercia, succeeded to her brothers' estates after their death, and by order of the King was married to Yvon Taylbois,[1] by whom she had no

[1] Ivo de Tailgebosc is said to have been Count of Anjou, which is false; he was a wood-tollman, and a plebeian. He came over with the Conqueror, married Lucia, daughter of

Appendices.

offspring. Countess Lucia, in the time of Henry I., married Roger, son of Gerald Romara, and had a son named William, afterwards Earl of his father's estates, and Earl of Lincoln. She was married a third time in the reign of King Stephen to Ralph, Earl of Chester, and had a son Ralph, afterwards Earl of Chester. Lucia is buried at Spalding.

William de Romara, founder of Revesby Abbey, had William de Romara, who died before his father, and was buried at Revesby. His father also in his last moments became a monk, and was buried at Revesby, after whose death William de Romara, the son of Lucia by her husband Roger, obtained from Roger de Romara, by favour of King Henry II., all the territory which belonged to William de Romara, his grandfather, and founded the Abbey of Clyve, and dying childless,[1] was buried at Revesby; and Ralph, Earl of Chester, his half-brother, obtained from King John his entire estate.

Revesby Abbey, Lincolnshire, was founded in 1142 by William de Romara, Earl of Lincoln.

Clyve, or Cliff, Cistercian Abbey, in Somersetshire, founded before A.D. 1188 by William de Romara, Earl of Lincoln.

Lappele, in Staffordshire, alien Priory of Black Monks, cell to the Abbey of St. Remigius of Reims, given by Algar III., Earl of Cheshire or Mercia, *temp*. Edward the Confessor.

Alfgar, Earl of East Anglia, with whom King William gave all the lands in Holland and Lincolnshire forfeited by Edwin and Morcar. He lived at Spalding. (See "History of Croyland Abbey.") He tried to deprive the monks of property given by Thorold, of Buckendale, with whom he claimed relationship, through his wife probably. Thorold was nearly related to Hereward's mother.—See "Domesday of Norfolk."

[1] This should be "without heirs male," for he had a daughter Rohais, or Hais, who in her own right inherited the title of Earl of Lincoln, and conferred it upon her husband, Gillebert de Gant (Ghent), A.D. 1149-1156. Her seal (*sigillum*), in the British Museum, has a Maltese cross ✠, and full-length figure in pointed oval shield. "In long dress with ornamental pattern, in right hand a lily (*luce*), in left fleur-de-lis."* Gilbert's name in seal 164 in British Museum is Gilbert Laci, Earl of Lincoln. The name Laci, with the lily (*luce*), and the title of Earl of Lincoln, point to descent from Lucia, sister of Edwin and Morcar. Henry Lacy, son of Gilbert Laci, or Lucy, had an only child and heiress, who married Thomas Earl of Lancaster, who became Earl of Lincoln through that marriage. He was eldest son of Edmund Crouchback, second son of King Henry III., and was beheaded (1322) by Edward II. for the part he nobly took in purging the kingdom of Piers Gaveston. Ghent, or Gant, in old Norman, was now spelt. Gaunt, and was attached to the Earldom of Lancaster, though rightly belonging to the Earl of Lincoln. The honours of Thomas of Lancaster devolved upon his brother Henry, whose only son, also Henry, was created Duke of Lancaster; his daughter and coheir, with her sister Maud, who died s.p., married John, third son of King Edward III., who became through his wife Duke of Lancaster, and with questionable right Hereward of the kingdom, in proof of which he claimed at the coronation of Richard II. the right of "bearing the sword," not as the King's brother, but in right of his wife, Blanche of Lancaster.

---

* Inscribed " Sigill. Hais Vxoris Gilleber E. Gant," from which it appears he was Earl of Ghent.

PUBLIC RECORD OFFICE.
ANCIENT DEEDS (DUCHY OF LANCASTER).
L. 38 (*Translation*).

"W[illiam] de Roumara to all his barons and men, French and English, of all England, greeting. Know ye that I have given to Robert,[1] grandson [or nephew] of the Countess,[2] the land of Ivo[3] and Colswain, his uncles, in fee and inheritance, and by the service of a fourth part of one knight. And this I grant to him for the soul of my mother, and for the service which the same Robert did to my mother. Witnesses: Robert Cantelupe, Reste the Chaplain, Herbert de Calz, Geoffrey Malabissa, Walter de Cantelupe,[4] Richard [of] Boulogne, Richard de Alvers, Hamon de Hauton, Baldry de Cales, Walter the Cook.

XIV.

ARMS OF A CONQUERED KNIGHT.

SOME thirty years ago a controversy on this subject arose in *Notes and Queries*. The question was asked: "What instances are there on record of the arms of a conquered knight being assumed by his victorious antagonist?" The following two instances were given in reply:

1. From Fuller's "Worthies of England," vol. i., p. 582: "Thomas Fisher, *alias* Hawkins, being a collonel under the Duke of Somerset in Musleborough [Musselburgh] Field, behaved himself right valiantly, and took a Scotchman prisoner who bore a griffin for his Arms. Whereupon the said Duke conferred on him the Arms of his captive, to be borne within a Border Varrey in relation to a prine coat which the said Duke (the granter thereof) quartered as descended from the Lord Beauchamp."

2. "Sir Robert Carey, knight (3rd series, vol. vi., pp. 483, 540), in person so valorous and skilful in arms that few presumed to enter the lists with him. Amongst his other exploits is recorded his triumph over an Arragonese knight in Smithfield, upon which occasion he was knighted and allowed to adopt the arms of his vanquished rival, namely, '3 roses on a bend.'"—From Burke's "Extinct and Dormant Peerage," 1831, p. 109 (Walter Rye, 3rd series, voL vi., pp. 313, 401).

It is, however, stated by Stafford Carey (p. 313, 3rd. S. vi., Oct. 15, 1864), that the arms referred to, "argent, on a bend sable, 3 roses of the first," were used by the Carey family (Sir John Carey) before the birth of the said Robert, and Mr. Robert Dymond supports him (p. 5403, series vi.). A correspondent adds: "Customs such as 'arms in use,' or others said to be 'from time whereof the memory of man runneth not to the contrary,' must date back to

---

[1] This Robert was probably son of Robert Fitzgerald, brother of the husband of Countess Lucia, Roger Fitzgerald.
[2] Roger Fitzgerald (de Roumara), William's father, married Countess Lucia.
[3] Presumably Ivo de Taillebois, called his uncle, having been the husband of the countess, who is called his aunt, his father Robert having been her brother-in-law.
[4] Afterwards Bishop of Worcester.

Appendices.

Richard I., when there is a prescriptive right to arms proceeding on the legal presumption of an original grant, and in such cases the Heralds' College can grant confirmation to individuals proving right of descent." The fact is, the "Laws of Arms" were in a primitive and uncodified condition even in France until after the capture of Jerusalem by the Crusaders. Hereward assumed the family bearing of an "eagle displayed," and added to it the "field chequy or and azure" of De Warrenne after his victorious combat with Frederick.

XV.

SHERIFF HUTTON CASTLE, YORKSHIRE.

THE historical castle of Sheriff Hutton, in Yorkshire, belonged to Richard of Gloucester, afterwards Richard III. It is a strongly built castle, eleven miles north of York, standing on the top of an eminence, its massive corner towers each containing a dungeon beneath the rooms, its windows, pierced through walls ten feet thick, looking from their height into the distant forest of Galtrees to the west, then a tract of wood, moor, and bog, spreading for many miles into the North Riding.

Here Anthony Woodville, Earl Rivers, who signed himself M. Nvlle (Neville or Neufville) la Vault Ærivieres, was confined for two months before he was consigned to Pontefract, where he was executed for his loyal devotion to the House of Lancaster and the poor little princes who were murdered in the Tower. In Shakespeare's tragedy, as he sees the wraiths of his victims pass before him, retribution haunts the wicked king. The ghost of Earl Rivers is conspicuous, and foretells his death:

> "Let me sit heavy on thy soul to-morrow,
> Rivers, that died at Pomfret [Pontefract]! Despair, and die!"

The young Earl of Warwick, son of the murdered Duke of Clarence, brother of Edward IV., who had married the daughter of the late Earl of Warwick, slain at Barnet in the Barons' war, was imprisoned at Sheriff Hutton Castle until sent by Henry VII. to the Tower of London.

XVI.

ESTATE OF CLEMENT HEREWARD, 1360, BARNINGHAMS.

BARNINGHAM HALL subsequently came into the hands of the Pastons, who have full information of its history. The mansion was built by the de Barningham family.

In 1312 Sir Henry de Seagrave, Kt., and his followers, came to the manor-house, and pricked the mother of William de Barningham with swords and cut her with knives to make her tell them of her jewels, money, and plate. The king, a very bad one (Edward II.), pardoned this recreant knight when indicted for the offence.

The estate came into possession of the Herewards about 1360, and is mentioned in the will of Clement Hereward, M.P. for Norfolk, 1426. About the end of this century, or later, it was sold to Sir Edward Paston and entailed on his eldest son. It was sold in 1757 to William Russell. A fatality seems to rest upon Norfolk estates, accentuated during the present century by agricultural depression.

SUPPLEMENTARY NOTES.

1. *Carucate of Land.*

CARUE de terre. Master Skene saith "That it containeth as great a portion of land as may be eyred [traversed] and tilled in a yeare and a day with one plough, which also is called a Hild or Hide of Land." Alfred the Great's monastery at Winchester is called Hyde from the area of the "Hide Mead" upon which it was built. The endowment of 27,000 acres in Hampshire and adjacent counties is all detached land.

2. *Office of Ward or Warden.*

The ancient office of Hereward, sword-guardian, or guardian of the army, is long anterior to the establishment of the English Parliament, but the importance of a wardenship may be gathered from the number of Acts of Parliament constituting or confirming such offices. Thus:

Warden of the King's Wardrobe created by Act of Parliament, Anno 5 Hen. III., Stat. 5.
Wardens of the Peace, 2 Ed. III., cap. 3.
Warden of the King's Armour in the Tower, 1 Ed. IV., cap. 1.
Warden of the Aulnage (Almonry), 18 Hen. VI., cap. 16.
Warden Courts, 31 Hen. VI., cap. 3.
Warden of the Marches, 4 Hen. VII., cap. 8.
Warden of the West Marches, Camden's "Britannia," page 606.
Warden of the Forest, Manwood, part i., pages 111, 112.
Wardens of the Fellowships in London, 14 Hen. VIII., cap. 2.

"Ward" or "warden" has the same signification as the French *gard*, *gardein*, or *gardien*, and was spelt in Saxon *vard* or *uuard*. Hereward is spelt in some old writings Hereuuard (see Domesday Book of Warwickshire). "Ward" implies the custody of a person or thing by office. The necessity for the consent of Parliament to the offices enumerated was on account of salaries, fees, or taxes attached to them.

3. *Hereward Seals in the British Museum.*

Besides the very important seal of Rohais, dau. of William de Roumara, and wife of Earl "Gillebert" of "Gant," the following seals are indexed:

9753. Herward, Christopher.
9753. Herward, George.
14692. Herward, John.

15544. Herward, John.
78 G 35. Herward, Roger.
85 T 22-31. Herward, Symon.
86 C 48. Hereward ⎫
          Herwar ⎭
78 T 50. Harward, Robert.

4. Earl Alfgar, described as Earl of Chester or Mercia, *temp.* of Edward the Confessor, endowed an alien priory of Black Monks at Lappele in Staffordshire. It was a cell to the Abbey of St. Remigals at Reims.

5. The Danish biographical tract on Hereward referred to in the Preface is catalogued as:

Fortælling om
Hervard Lourikson
Copenhagen.
Karl Schonbergs Forlag, 1865.

Copies are very scarce.

6. Domesday Book records that Earl Edwin's estate at (Ladbroc) Ladbroke, Warwickshire, was also held by Hereward, and for a time by his godfather, "Gislebert of Gant." Also that Hereward's estate at Merst n or Marston, had been previously held of Earl Alfgar. Some of these lands are recorded as in possession of Turchil, of Warwick, who was vice-comes, or Sheriff of Mercia, under Leofric, and he probably held the lands *ad interim* until Hereward's claim was decided. Turchil held aloof from Harold, and was confirmed in his estates and offices by William. Earl Gilbert, of Ghent, had great weight and influence in England in the reign of Edward the Confessor and subsequently. He had not only landed estates in fourteen counties, but, at a time when mills were generally a monopoly of the Crown, he had no less than five mills at his manor of Empingham, in Lincolnshire, and one at (Folchingham) Falkingham. He also had five mills of the King's Soke in Rutland, besides an immense number of slaves, villeins, sokemen, and bordars. On many of his manors there was a church. The wapentake of Gartree in Lincolnshire was previously known as Haverstoe or Harwardeshov.

7. *Wills and Bequests.*

The following extract of the will of Clement Harward, dated Nov. 15, 1586, is given as a good specimen of such documents of that period. It is not the will of the head of the family, who was Herward, or Harward, of Boton Hall and Pensthorpe:

"I Clement Harward of Aldburgh co. Norff. Esq[r]—My bodye to be buried in Aldburgh Church amongst my ancestors, if I die in Norff. Item I will & devise that Eleanor my well beloved wife, shall during her natural life have, use, and take the profits of all my manors, houses, lands, & I further will and devise that if I die without heir male of my body lawfullie begotten that then Robert Harwarde the son of John Harwarde of Boton, gent. shall after the death of said Eleanor my wife have as well all & singular such my manors &c.—To have and to hold all & singular the premises to the said Rob. Harwarde & to the heirs male of his body lawfully begotten, remainder to Thos. Harwarde son of John Harwarde of Poole in the County of Dorset gent. & to the heirs male of his body lawfully begotten; remainder to my cousin Gilbert Parker of Honynge in the co. of Norf. gent. & to the heirs male of his body &c.; remainder to my cosen Robert Thetforde of Catts in the said co. of Norf. with power of jointure to the said Robt Harward to the value of £40 yearly; to my sister Barbara Revett £5—to my sister Catherine my house &c. called Edymans; to my sister Anne Harward £20;—to my cosen James Winter 20^s a year for life; also I give and bequeath to my wife all my plate her apparell & jewels, & 3 carpets which she brought with her to her house at Cranworth."

The terms of this will are much more clear and concise than the wills made 200 years later, which covered many folios. James Winter, a cousin, was a descendant of Ibe Winter, Hereward's trusty companion in 1066-69.

8. *The Herewards' Refusal to take part in Civil Wars.*

It must not be supposed that the abstention of the Saxon leaders in England from internecine conflicts, in which the people always suffered more severely than the descendants of the Norman lords, was occasioned by any falling off in prowess or bravery. It was not the knights or Norman men-at-arms who gained the great victories at Creçy, Poictiers, and Agincourt, but the irresistible English archers, the descendants of the good patriots of the Bruneswald and Sherwood Forest, under their Saxon leaders, the men typified by Hereward and his gallant band in the eleventh century.

9. *Status of Aldermen.*

"Ægaldermon," "Alderman," or "Elderman" answered to the French *seigneur* and Italian *signor* (senior).

10. *Oslac, and his Family.*

Oslac, cupbearer to King Ethelwulf, was a scion of the royal house of the Jutes, settled in the Isle of Wight. He was the father of Osburh, or Osburgha, wife of King Ethelwulf, and mother of Alfred the Great. Two of his sons had been murdered by Ceadwalla. Duke Oslac, in Edgar's reign, is said by all historians to have been a descendant of the cupbearer. He was appointed by Edgar to the government of Deira, the northern province of England, extending from the Tyne to the Humber. He was, however, banished by Edward the Martyr, owing to the intrigues of Alderman Elfhere. He is described in the chronicles as "the beloved hoary-headed hero."

11. *Freeman, and the Norman Conquest.*

Freeman's "Norman Conquest" is a great work, but in the depths of its serious and correct history there is a trace of romance ever revealing itself when William of Normandy has to be discussed. Freeman's use of authorities is at times disingenuous; he contradicts himself in his account of Hereward, and his versions of facts are often strongly coloured with self-opinion. His work is an absolute glorification of the Norman intruders, and although himself of Saxon descent, he has little or nothing to urge in their behalf.

From 1037 it was a usual custom for the English of note, when expatriated, or from any cause obliged to leave their native country, to proceed to Bruges in Flanders. Thus Emma, the widowed Queen of Canute, Gunhild, his niece, and her two sons, Thurkill and Heming, Earl Godwin and his sons Swegen and Tostig, and finally Hereward, sought refuge with Baldwin, Earl or Marquis of Flanders, at the Court of Bruges. The importance of the trade in wool with England accounts for Baldwin's desire for friendly relations with England, and he thus secured the raw material which produced the great wealth of the gallant weavers in Ghent and other great burgher towns in the Low Countries. The state of the Continent at the period precluded the possibility of the rearing and maintenance of flocks of sheep.

12. *Hereward of Pebwith.*

Hereward of Pebwith, or Bedworth, co. Warwick. The head of the family was sometimes called and known as "de Bedeworth" from the estate which appears, from the grants recorded from it, to have been of considerable extent. In an extract from the Catalogue of Ancient Deeds in the Public Record Office we find:

"Warwick, B. 390. Grant by Hereward, son of Robert de Bedeworth, to Thomas de Flanville, of land (in Bedeworth). Witnesses: Michael de Bedeworth, Alan de Paylington, Gervase de Farncote, and others named."

(Seal.)

In a subsequent grant (Warwick, B. 407), dated Friday, Christmas Eve, 12 Rich. II., William Hereward, of Bedeworthe, grants to John, son of Simon le Fluron, of Bedeworth, "of land in the fields of Bedeworthe," "in Longecrone le Longcroft, echeles furlong, and Peshul."

Index.

ALDRETH CAUSEWAY, 38
 Ælfthryth, a Saxon lady, 41
Æthelwine, Bishop of Durham, 37
Alfgar banished (1052), 24
Alselin, or Ascelin Gouel de Perceval, 47
Ariovistus, 8
Arms of Alfred the Great, 66
 „ of Edward the Confessor, 67
 „ of Ethelred II., 67
 „ of the late Duke of Buckingham, 67

BATTLE ABBEY Roll, 64
 Bellamonte, Count of Mellent, Appendix III.
Bequest of Hereward's grandson, 48
Berkshire men join Camp of Refuge, 37
Bourne, owners of, in Domesday, 18
Bruges, capital of Flanders, 26
Buckingham, late Duke of, 62

CAMP of Refuge, 37
 "Chequy" coat of arms, origin of, 66
Civil Wars of the Roses, 30
Coleshill, Hereward's castle at, 46
College of Arms, 64
Chariovalda or Harivald, 7
Cheltenham, estates at, 79
Coins, Early English, 11
Compton, Bishop of Oxford, Appendix, 113
Coram Rege Rolls tampered with, 60
Coronation oath of William I., 31
Countess Lucia, 92, and Appendix XIII.
Cruelty of William I., Appendix II.
Curtmantle, 76, note

DANES as pagans, 84
 Danes Christianized, 84
Danish burial-places, 37
Danish troubles, 14
De Hereward, Theodore and William, 90
De Lascelles family, 59
Dugdale as an antiquary, 61
Dugdale, Sir William, Garter King at Arms, 110

EDWARD THE CONFESSOR, 22
 Edwin, Earl, death of, 36
Earl Edwin's fictitious pedigree, 67
Earldoms held by Hereward's ancestors, 82
Ealderman and Earl, 84
Ellis, Sir Henry's, evidence, 19
Emigration to Severn Valley, 91
Etymological changes, rules for, 50
Evermue, Hugh de, 88

FEN COUNTRY, described by Crabbe, 36
Flemings, character of, 26
Forest life, 40
Forest officers, 58
Freeman, Professor, partial and unsympathetic, 16
Freeman, Professor, slights Domesday record, 17

GILBERT OF GHENT, Hereward's godfather, 26
Gilbert of Ghent, Earl of Lincoln, 92
Godiva, wife of Leofric III., 86
Godwin and his sons hostile to Hereward's family, 24

Great Book of the church of Ely, 48
Greville, John, Sheriff of Glamorgan, 78
Greville, William, of Milcote, founder of Earl of Warwick's family, 78
Gruffydd, or Griffith, King of North Wales, 109
Gruffydd, ancestor of Henry VII., 87
Gruffydd marries Alfgar's daughter, 109

HAMILTON, descent of Dukes of, Appendix, 105
Hamond Claxton, 71
"Har," Scandinavian for Odin, or Woden, 53
Harvard, John, Appendix V.
Harvard of Southwark, Appendix, 106
Harward, Devon branch, 70, 71
Harward, William, of "Blakfreres," Appendix, 107
Hawarden Castle, Appendix VII.
Harwarde, Gregory of Redeham, 77
Harward, or Hereward, of Hartlebury, 95
Harward, Michael, key-table, 96
Harward of Bretforton, 49
Harward of Harvington, 97
Harward, Rev. J., key-table, 98
Harward, Dr. Richard, 72
Harwood, derivation of, 58
Hayward, or Haward, 59
Henry Howard, K.G., 61
Heralds, corruption of, 64
Heralds and fictitious pedigrees, 67
Heredity, 81
Hereward, Robert, Archdeacon of Taunton, 64
„ appointed Commissioner by Edward III., 68
„ William, Abbot of Cirencester, 64
„ Clement, M.P. for Norwich, 68
„ Robert, Sheriff co. Norfolk, 68
„ seals in British Museum, 69
„ Richard, marries Elizabeth Greville, 78
„ direct ancestor of last seventeen generations, 79
„ as Esquire, Appendix I.
„ or Harward, key-table, 93
„ of Merrow, Surrey, 77
„ time of Ethelbald, King of Mercia, 82

Hereward, anterior to Norman Conquest, 85
„ burial at Croyland Abbey, 87
„ in Norfolk, sketch pedigree, 94
„ almost forgotten, 2
„ lineage generally unknown, 5
„ etymology of, 7
„ mentioned by Tacitus, 7
„ Warden of the Sword, 8
„ settlement in Surrey, 9
„ „ in Oxfordshire, 13
„ relation to Leofric, Earl of Mercia, 18
„ corroborative proof of descent, 19
„ true nobility of, 20
„ self-abnegation of, 20
„ early training of, 21
„ strength of body and mind, 21
„ banished, not outlawed, 22
„ alleged offence of, 23
„ his trip to Flanders, 25
„ reception of in Flanders, 25
„ "vir strenuissimus," 27
„ knighted by Abbot Brand, 34
„ as a leader of men, 28
„ "the mirror of knighthood," 29
„ his return to England, 31
„ surprises Normans at Bourne, 31
„ at the Camp of Refuge, 35
„ disguises himself to reconnoitre, 38
„ strategy of, and military genius, 38
„ his fighting prowess, 38
„ compelled by treachery to retire, 39
„ his Saxon supporters, 39
„ carries on guerilla warfare, 40
„ acknowledges William's authority, 41
„ his lands restored, 41
„ marriage with Ælfthryth, 43
„ expedition to Maine, 45
„ tragic end in Gaimar's Chronicle, 46
„ more probable end in the "Gesta," 46, 89-98
„ serves William faithfully, 48
„ his lineal descendants, 48

Index. 127

Hereward, sometimes described as De Bedeworth, Appendix, 119
Herward, John, of Boton Hall, Norfolk, 73
"History of Norfolk," by W. Rye, 60
Howard, Huard, or Houard, 59
Howard, Duke of Norfolk, 59
  „ Earl of Effingham, 60
  „ Earl of Carlisle, 60
Howard claim, Appendix VIII.
Howardus in Domesday, 60

INGULPH, how far worthy of credence, 4
Ireland, people of, devoted to Edward the Confessor, 25

KINGSBURY HALL, Warwickshire, 45
Kingsley's "Hereward the Wake," Appendix IX.
Kingsley, Rev. C., 62
Knights Templars, powers of, 62
Knights of the Bath, dress prescribed for, 72

LANCASTER, Duchy of, Appendix XI.
Leofric III., Earl of Mercia, 13
Le Palmere of Francton, 80
Liber Ecclesia Eliensis, 90
Lille, castle of, 26
Llandaff, Lord Bishop of, 96
Lucia, Countess, 92; Appendix XIII.

MANNING AND BRAY, account of Harwardis leag, Surrey, 9
Marle, residence of Earls of Flanders, 26
Milcote, near Weston-on-Avon, 78
Morkery Woods, 18, note

NETHERTON, S., Esq., 96
Norfolk, Dukes of, Earls Marshal of England, 61
Norfolk estates of Herewards, 77
Norman Invasion, 30
  „ witchcraft, 38
Norman and Saxon jealousy, 76

OGER THE BRETON, 39
Oppression of the Saxons, 32
Orthography of Hereward, 50
Oslac, noble Danish house, 14, 19
Owen of Orielton, 96

PALMERSTON, the late Lord, 62
Pebworth, Pebwith, or Bedeworth, 45
Plunder of the Saxons, 32
Pocahontas at Boton Hall, 73, note
Prefix "de," note, p. 56
Progress, so-called, 74

RALPH DE DOL, 46
References, 83
Roger le Bigod, Appendix IV.
Rogers, Alderman, of Stratford-on-Avon, Appendix, 107
Roumara of Revesby, 92

ST. MARY OF ABINGDON, 37
Saturday Review, 63, note
Saxon history, dearth of, 5
  „ occupations, 11
  „ settlements, 9
  „ society, 11
  „ "tun," or town, 12
Sheriff Hutton Castle, 46
Simon de Montfort, Appendix, 105
Strekingham, battle of, 86
Stuart dynasty, events of, 30
Suevi, The, 8

TAILLEBOIS, Ivo de, 34, 40
Tamworth Castle, 20
Terrington, or Taunton, Norfolk, 49
Temple, Sir Grenville, 62
Thorold, Abbot of Malmesbury, 35
Treachery of monks of Ely, 39
Trial by battle, 34
Torfrida, the lady, 29
  „ at the Court of Bruges, 29
  „ her accomplishments, 30

VISCOUNTESS COBHAM, 67

WAKE OF COURTEEN HALL, Northamptonshire, 63
"Wake," origin of, 63
Warwickshire branch, pedigree of, 91
Wheeler of Winterfold, 96
Wilburga, heiress of Terrington, 89
William, at Castle of Cambridge, 37
  „ perjured himself, 31
Witan of Kent, prayer to Æthelstan, 24
Woden's wagon, 8
Woodland, extent of, 39
Wulfstan, Bishop of Worcester, 41
Wygenhale, Sir William de, 60

Elliot Stock, Paternoster Row, London.

www.ingramcontent.com/pod-product-compliance
Lightning Source LLC
Chambersburg PA
CBHW031504160426
43195CB00010BB/1098